Cue for Communication

Shiona Harkess and John Eastwood

Oxford University Press
1981

Oxford University Press, Walton Street, Oxford OX2 6DP

London Glasgow New York Toronto
Delhi Bombay Calcutta Madras Karachi
Kuala Lumpur Singapore Hong Kong Tokyo
Nairobi Dar Es Salaam Cape Town Salisbury
Melbourne Wellington
and associate companies in
Beirut Berlin Ibadan Mexico City

ISBN 0 19 432781 7
© Harkess & Eastwood 1981

Acknowledgements
Photographs by Dafydd Jones
Illustrations by Colin Smithson
The authors would like to thank Cassell and Co. Ltd.
for their permission to use the extracts on page 28 from
The Book of Lists by Wallechinsky, Wallace and Wallace.

The Publishers would like to thank the following
for permission to reproduce photographs:
Barnaby's Picture Library, British Tourist Authority,
Camera Press, The Kobal Collection.

The would also like to thank the following
for their co-operation:

Alitalia, Cathay Pacific, Playhouse, Oxford,
Royal Festival Hall, Scamps.

Set in Compugraphic Bembo by
T. H. Brickell & Son Ltd, The Blackmore Press,
Shaftesbury, Dorset
Printed in Hong Kong

Contents

Introduction

This book is for upper secondary school or adult learners of English as a foreign language. It is most suitable for students at an intermediate or advanced level.

The material

The book contains material for practising a wide range of communicative functions (such as asking for information or giving an opinion) in a meaningful context. The context is provided by a map, diagram, table, list or series of pictures on each left-hand page. On each right-hand page there is a list of the main exponents of the function, followed by models for oral practice. There is an Appendix at the end of the book with suggestions for more open-ended practice of each function, references to the companion volume *Cue for a Drill* (where further structural practice can be found) and keys to the illustrations where necessary. The material can be used to teach new functions, to teach the communicative use of a particular item of grammar, or for revision and extra practice in communication. An important aspect of the material is that, after initial guidance from the teacher, each practice can be carried out by the students themselves without intervention from the teacher.

How to use the material

Step 1
The functions dealt with are listed in the Contents and in the Index. The teacher finds the material on the function he/she wants the class to practise.

Step 2
The students look at the visual in their books, and the teacher explains any unknown words.

Step 3
The students look at the list of exponents at the top of the right-hand page and practise saying sentences with each exponent, e.g. on page 76 'I like riding/golf' etc. The teacher can give examples first, and should point out the differences between exponents where necessary, e.g. that 'I'm very keen on . . .' is more enthusiastic than 'I like . . .'; that, on page 36, 'I'm afraid I disagree' is more formal than 'Rubbish'.

Step 4
The teacher says the first part of each model in the Practice, e.g. 'How about going sailing?' and a student replies e.g. 'Yes, I like sailing.' or (if he/she does not like sailing) 'But I don't like sailing'. The teacher says several sentences using the same pattern as in the first sentence of the model but substituting, in random order, elements from the left-hand page, e.g. 'How about going climbing/a game of tennis?' Students should react naturally and give their own opinion or express their real feelings whenever possible.

Step 5
The students work in pairs. This is the most valuable stage of the Practice and should begin as soon as possible. The teacher should aim to have everyone in the class practising the communicative function. If the teacher feels an intermediate stage is necessary, the students can say the first part of the model and the teacher reply before going on to pair work.

Step 6
The practice material is primarily oral, but there are cases where a function might well occur in writing, e.g. an opinion (p. 34) can be expressed in a letter to a newspaper. In such cases a short written practice would be appropriate, e.g. I think adverts are a waste of money/It seems to me that if we want industry, we must have pollution.

Step 7
The activity suggested in the Appendix can be used to give practice in a less controlled context. The intention here is that students should go beyond the context of the practice material and achieve true communication by performing a function in a more natural situation. If they need further practice of a particular structure, references are given to the companion volume *Cue for a Drill*, which provides contextualized practice of structures.

Actors

Actresses

Singers

Politicians

Identification of people

Asking about identity
Who's that . . . ?
What's the name of that . . . ?
Do you know who that (. . .) is?
Do you recognize that . . .?

Checking identity
Is that . . .?
Isn't that . . .?
So that's . . ., is it?
That's . . ., isn't it?

Identifying
That's . . .
(Yes,) I think that's . . . (but I'm not sure).
Er. Well, it/he/she might be . . .
(No,) I'm not certain. Perhaps it's/he's/she's . . .

Not identifying
(I'm) sorry, I don't know.
(I'm afraid) I've no idea (who that is).
I haven't a clue (who it/he/she is) (, I'm afraid).
I don't recognize him/her.
I know his/her face, but I've no idea what his/her name is.

Practice A
Who's that actress in the middle ?
That's Sophia Loren.

What's the name of that actor on the right?
I haven't a clue, I'm afraid.

Do you recognize that singer on the left?
Yes, I think that's Joan Baez.

Practice B
Isn't that Mrs Ghandi on the left?
Yes, I believe it is.

Is that Jane Fonda on the right?
I think so.

That's Mrs Thatcher in the middle, **isn't it?**
I'm afraid I don't know.

Telephone Numbers

Miss Benson, Elmhayes School 25750

Mrs Hutchins, Wessex Hotel 24394

Helen Fraser, DBM International 84049

Angela Mears, Home Farm 29224

Eric Hill, Brookway Garage 30451

Mr Ali, Queen's Hotel 48624

Mr Vickers, Stanford + Co 71230

Alan Nash, West End College 77937

Jill Farrant, Safeway Insurance 31192

Mr Saville, Buywell Supermarket 42002

Identification on the telephone

When answering
(Alan) Nash (speaking/here).
The Wessex Hotel.
Two four three nine four.

When calling
My name's Alan Nash.
Alan (Nash) speaking/here.
This is Alan Nash (speaking).

Asking for identification
Who's calling/speaking?
Who am I speaking to?
Could I have your name (please)?
Is that the Wessex Hotel?
Is that (you) Angela?
Mr Ali?

Identifying who you want to speak to
Could I speak to Alan (Nash)/Mr Nash please?
(I'd like to speak to) Mr Ali please.
Is Angela in/there (please)?

Practice A
Elmhayes School.
Ah, good morning. **Miss Benson please.**
Two nine double two four.
Oh, hello. **Is Angela in please?**

Practice B
West End College.
Good morning. **Could I speak to** Mr Nash please?
Who's calling?
[*name of student*]

Practice C
Safeway Insurance. Can I help you?
Yes please. **I'd like to speak to** Miss Farrant.
Who's calling?
[*name of student*].
Hello! **Jill Farrant here.**
Oh, hello Jill! **This is** [*name of student*] **speaking.**

Cars

  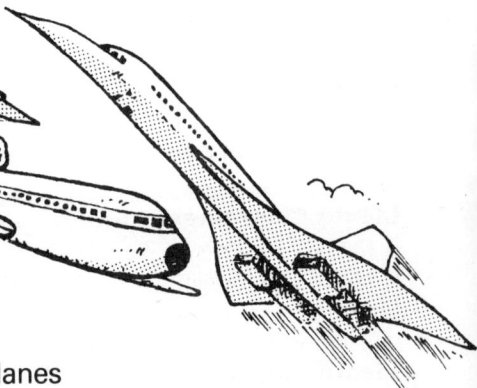

Planes

Birds

Instruments

Identification of things

Asking about identity
See that . . .? What (make) is it?
Do you know what (make) that (. . .) is?
What sort/kind/make of . . . is the one . . .?
What on earth is that (. . .)?
Which of those . . . is a(n) . . .?

Checking identity
Is that . . .?
Isn't that . . .?
So that is . . ., is it?
That's . . ., isn't it?

Identifying things
(Yes.) (I think) it's a . . .
(I'm not sure/certain.) It might/could be a . . .
Maybe/Perhaps it's a . . .
(No.) The one . . ., (I think).

Not identifying
(I'm sorry, I don't know (what it is).
(I'm afraid) I've no idea.
I haven't a clue/I haven't the faintest (idea) (, I'm afraid).
God knows!

Practice A
See that plane on the right? **What is it?**
It's a Concorde.

Do you know what that car in the middle **is?**
I'm not certain. It could be a Citroen.

What on earth is that bird on the left?
God knows!

Practice B
Which of those instruments **is a** saxophone?
I haven't the faintest, I'm afraid.

So that car on the right **is a** Volkswagen, **is it?**
No. The one on the left is a Volkswagen.

Mr David Kerr

Mrs Jean Wilson

Mr Kenneth Smart

Miss Margaret Allen

Mr Joe Kaduna

Mrs Emily Brown

Mr Alan West

Miss Alison Jones

Mr Bill Smith

Description of people

Asking for a description
What does . . . look like?
Tell me what . . . looks like.
Could you describe . . . for me?
What kind of person would you say he/she . . . is?
How tall/old is . . .?
How does . . . dress?
How . . . would you say . . . was/is?

Describing people
He's/She's (rather/pretty/quite/very/not at all) . . . (actually).
He/She has/'s got . . .
His/Her . . . is/are . . .
He's/She's rather/a little/a bit (on the) . . . (side).
He/She must be (just) over/getting on for/about forty/six foot.
He's/She's of average height/build.
He/She (often/never/always) wears/dresses . . .
He's always in . . .
He/She (always/never) looks . . . (enough) (to me).
He/She looks (very/quite/rather) like . . .

Practice A
What does Kenneth Smart **look like?**
He's rather attractive **actually. He's** tall, well-built and **must be just
over** forty. **He's got** dark hair and a handsome face and **he's always in**
casual clothes.

Could you describe Margaret Allan?
She's got a very good figure and beautiful long black hair. **She dresses**
well and **always wears** beautiful jewelry.

Practice B
How old **would you say** Alan West **is?**
He must be getting on for sixty.
And **what kind of person would you say he is?**
Well, **he looks** pleasant **enough to me.**

How old **would you say** David Kerr **is?**
He must be over sixty.
And **what kind of person would you say he is?**
Well, **he's rather** quiet, **actually.**

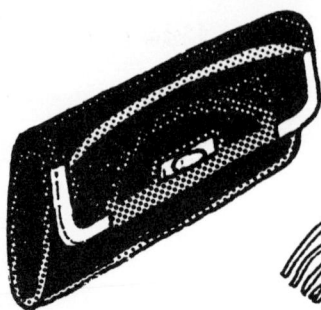

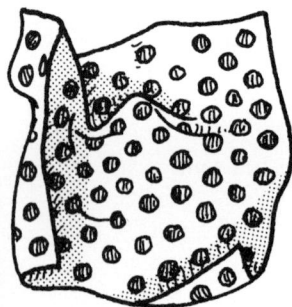

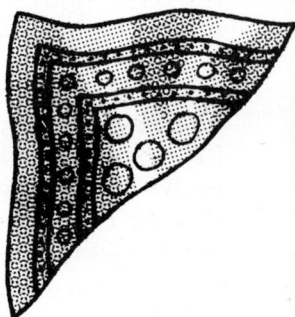

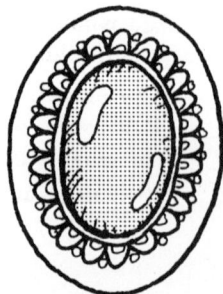

Description of things

Asking for a description
What's it like?
What does it look like?
What kind/type/sort (of . . .) (is it)?
What colour/shape is it?
How big/small is it?
Could you describe it for me? Is there anything . . . about it?

Describing things
It's quite/rather/fairly/very . . .
It's . . .-shaped.
It's made of . . .
It's got . . . on . . .
It's . . . with . . .
The unusual thing about it is that it . . .
It looks . . . (but it's not).
It looks like a . . . (but it's not).

Practice A
I've got a new watch.
Oh, have you? **What's it like?**
Well, **it's** gold **with** a black leather bracelet.
Nice!

I've got a new scarf.
Oh, have you? **What kind?**
Well, **it's** a triangular cotton one **with** a red and white pattern.
Nice!

Practice B
Has anyone seen my handbag?
What does it look like?
It's a shoulder bag **with** a fringe.
No, sorry.

Has anyone seen my brooch?
What does it look like?
It's small and **star-shaped.**
Sorry.

How electricity is made

Oil, coal or uranium fuels a boiler or reactor.

The boiler or reactor produces steam.

The steam drives a turbine.

The turbine turns a generator.

The generator produces electricity.

A transformer increases the current.

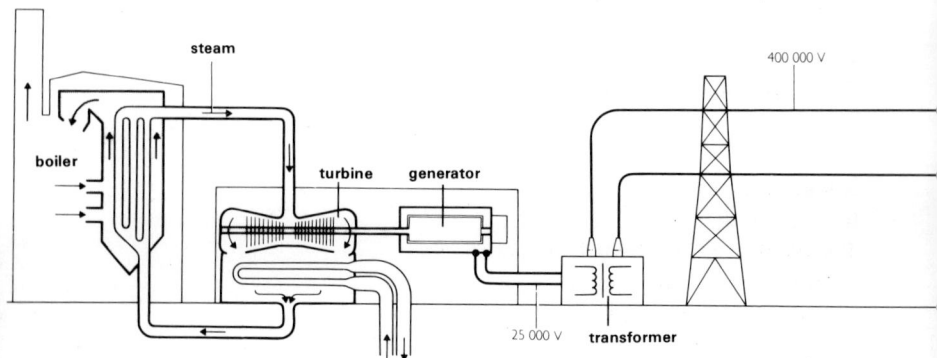

steam

boiler

turbine

generator

400 000 V

25 000 V

transformer

Transmission lines carry the electricity over long distances.

A sub-station reduces the current.

Underground cables supply buildings with electricity.

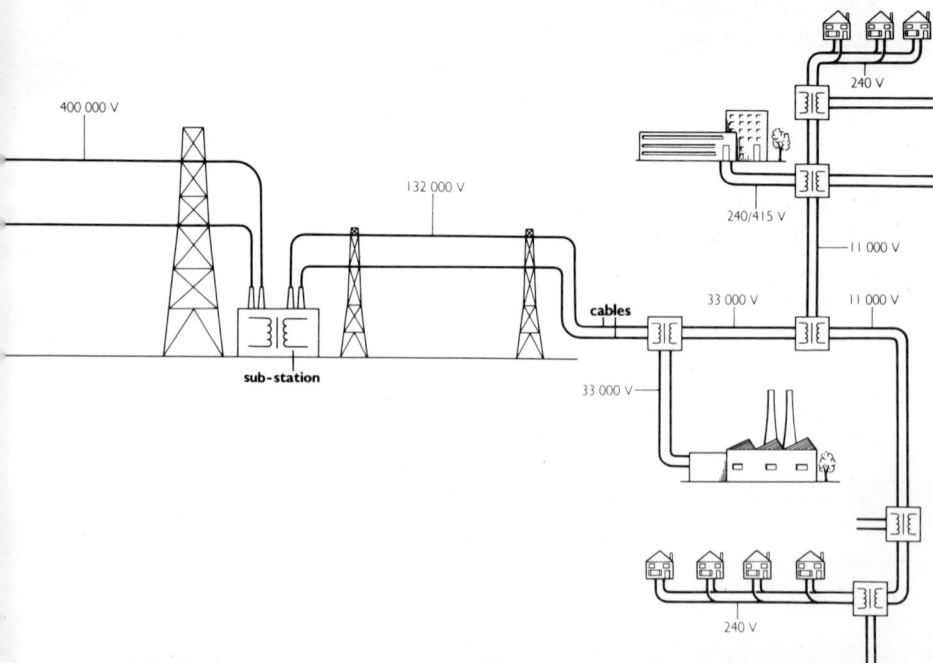

400 000 V

132 000 V

sub-station

cables

240 V

240/415 V

11 000 V

33 000 V

11 000 V

11 000 V

33 000 V

240 V

Description of a process

Asking about a process
Could you explain how it works?
How does . . . work?
What does . . . do?
How/At what stage/When is . . . produced?
How/At what stage does it produce . . .?
What happens first/next/then/after that?
Then what (happens)?

Describing a process
(When/As/Before/After . . .,) . . . is produced/fuelled etc. (by . . .).
This/It produces/turns etc. . . .
Basically/The basic principle is that . . .

Checking you understand a process
So that's . . ., is it?
So that produces . . ., does it?
Let me just check I've understood/got it right. (First) . . .
So if I've understood correctly, that must be . . .

Practice A
What happens first?
A reactor **is fuelled.**
Then what happens?
It produces steam.

Practice B
When is the current **increased?**
Before the electricity **is carried** over long distances.

At what stage is steam **produced?**
As the reactor **is fuelled.**

Practice C
So that's the generator, **is it?**
That's right. **It produces** the electricity.

Now, **let me just check I've got it right.** The transformer **increases** the current and the sub-station **reduces** it.
That's right. **It's increased before it's carried** over long distances and **it's reduced before** buildings **are supplied** with it.

Telephone Messages

Mr Brooks – Delivering the carpet soon.

Julia – She's borrowed the car.

Mr Thompson – Are you going to the party?

Peter – Don't order the furniture yet.

Mrs Grant – Will call to see you about the holiday soon.

Mr Jones – Where are the records?

Miss White – Could you send the cheque?

Mr Jackson – The match has been cancelled.

Betty – Do you want the tickets?

Bill – Can't find the book.

Mrs Gardiner – Please phone her about the concert as soon as possible.

Robert – Have you spoken to Mr Henderson about joining the club?

Messages

Passing on statements
. . . said/told me/left a message (that) . . .
. . . called (in)/phoned/wrote to tell you/say (that) . . . ·
Apparently . . .

Passing on questions
Could you let . . . know if/whether . . . (or not).
Could you let . . . know where/when etc. . . .
. . . asked/wanted to know/enquired/was wondering . . .
. . . rang (up)/came (in)/wrote to ask (you) . . .

Passing on commands and requests
(Apparently/ . . . says) you are (not) to . . .
. . . told/asked/requested you (not) to . . .
. . . asked if you could (possibly) . . .
. . . asked if you would mind . . .
. . . asked if it would be all right for him/her to . . .
. . . was wondering/asked if he/she could . . .

Practice A
Did Mr Brooks call while I was out?
Yes. **He called to say** he's delivering the carpet soon.

Did Mr Jackson ring while I was out?
Yes. **Apparently** the match has been cancelled.

Practice B
Did Mr Thompson ring while I was out?
Yes. **Could you let him know if** you're going to the party **or not?**

Did Mr Jones leave a message while I was out?
Yes. **He was wondering** where the records were.

Practice C
Did Peter ring while I was out?
Yes. **He says you're not to** order the furniture yet.

Did Miss White leave a message while I was out?
Yes. **She asked you to** send the cheque.

People	Problem	Solution
Chemco	dumping of chemicals	provide alternative dumping site
	leakage of chemicals	repair works
	poisonous waste	process waste
	chemicals spilt in motor accidents	strengthen containers
Local residents	unprocessed farmyard waste	move animals
	sileage heap	move sileage
	disposal of motor oil down drains	burn waste oil
	domestic oil spilling and leaking	move and repair tank
	discharge of oil from boats	patrol river regularly
Local council	waste from inefficient sewage works	modernize sewage works
Gasol Co.	oil slicks from frequent tanker accidents on narrow road	re-route tankers or widen road

Reports

Reporting complaints
. . . (have) complained about/that . . .
. . . are (very much) against . . .
. . . are angry/furious/concerned/worried about . . .

Reporting suggestions
. . . proposed/suggested (that) . . . should . . .
. . . suggested doing . . .
. . . were/are for doing . . .

Reporting conflicts
Whereas . . ., . . .
. . ., but . . . .
Although . . ., . . .
. . . refuse to . . .
. . . can see . . . point, but feel (that) . . .
. . . have threatened to/will (not) . . . unless . . .
There is no way . . . will go along with/agree to . . .
. . . still insist on/that . . .

Reporting reconciliations
(As . . . have offered to . . .,) . . . have agreed to . . .
. . . have agreed to . . . as long as . . .
. . . are prepared to comply/go along with . . .
. . . will co-operate if/as long as . . .

Practice A
The local residents **are very concerned about** the leakage of chemicals from Chemco's premises.
Are they? Well, Chemco **are concerned about** the farmyard waste.

The local residents **are for** Gasol re-routing their tankers.
Are they? Well, Gasol **are for** the Council widening the road.

Practice B
Why can't the Council and the local residents reach an agreement?
The local residents **refuse to** move their animals.

So the Council and Gasol have come to an agreement?
Yes. The Council **have agreed to** widen the road.

London-Bombay

Depart London, Heathrow Airport, Terminal 3
(Minimum check-in time 60 mins.
BA First class 45 mins)
Arrive Bombay, Santa Cruz Airport

Frequency	Aircraft Dep	Arr	Via	Flight	Aircraft
MO	1015*	0520+	PARIS FRANKFURT KUWAIT	A1116	747
MO	1545*	1215+	MOSCOW, TEHERAN DELHI	A1516	707
MO	1600*	0745+	BAHRAIN	BA814	747
TU	0905*	0050+	BAHRAIN	BA824	747
TU	1015*	0400+	PARIS, ROME	A1102	747
WE	1015*	0455+	ROME, DELHI	A1104	747
WE	1210*	0340+	DOHA	BA730	VCX
WE	1700*	1330+	MOSCOW, TEHERAN DELHI	A1504	707
TH	1015*	0625+	PARIS FRANKFURT DELHI	A1106	747
TH	1500*	0720+	ROME	BA888	747
TH	1845*	1100+	ROME	A1126	747
FR	0935*	0450+	CAIRO, DELHI	A1118	707
FR	1015*	0815+	PARIS FRANKFURT KUWAIT, DELHI	A1108	747
FR	1830*	1015+	BAHRAIN	BA888	747

* One hour later from 19 Mar
+ Next day

Requests for information

Starting an enquiry
(Excuse me.) Can/Could you tell me . . .?
          Do you know . . .?
          I wonder if you could tell me . . .
          I wonder if you could help me. I'm looking for/I need
          some information on . . .
Could I just ask . . .?
(Just) one question . . .?

Enquiring
Is/Does/Can etc. . . . (or . . .)?
Where/How many/What kind of . . .? etc.
Who can I ask/Who knows about . . .?

Practice A
Can I stop off in Rome on Flight BA 888?
Yes, you can.

When does Flight BA 814 arrive in Bombay?
At seven forty-five on Tuesday morning.

Practice B
Excuse me. Can you tell me if there's a flight to Bombay on
Monday?
Yes, there are three. Would you like to leave in the morning or the
afternoon?
In the afternoon, please. **What time** do they leave?
At fifteen forty-five and sixteen hours.

Excuse me. Do you know if there's a flight to Bombay on Tuesday?
Yes, there are two. Would you like to fly British Airways or Air India?
Air India, please. **Where** does the flight stop?
At Paris and Rome.

Practice C
Here's your ticket to Doha. You're leaving at twelve ten on Wednesday
and you arrive at three forty the following morning.
Fine. **Just one question. What**'s my flight number?
BA 730.

Here's your ticket to Bahrain. You're leaving at nine five on Tuesday on
flight BA 824.
Fine. **Could I just ask** when I arrive?
At ten to one the following morning.

Comfortable hotels

All hotels are licensed unless otherwise shown. Star ratings are those of the AA or RAC.

🛏	+ Number = No. of bedrooms
🛁	Rooms with private bath/shower and own toilet
G	Groundfloor rooms available
↕	Lift
UL	Unlicensed
⚲	Games room

TV	TV provided in bedrooms
TV C	Colour TV provided in the bedrooms
TV	TV lounge
R	Radio in the bedrooms
☎	Telephone in the bedrooms
☕	Tea/Coffee making facilities in bedrooms
☕	Room Service
▥	Central Heating in bedrooms

THE GEORGE—4-star hotel overlooking sea. Amenities include sauna suite, gymnasium and hairdressing salon.

🛏 120 🛁 120 G ↕ TV R ☎ ▥ ☕

THE SHIP INN—3-star hotel in central level sea front position. Coffee shop open all day.

🛏 75 🛁 40 ↕ TV C R ☎ ☕ ▥ ⚲

REGENT'S PALACE—3-star hotel on the sea front in 3 acres of gardens. Amenities include sauna, solarium suite and hairdressing salon.

🛏 77 🛁 51 G ↕ TV R ☕ ▥ ⚲

WHITE HART—3-star hotel in own gardens, near to cliff lift, sea, shops and entertainments. Regular weekend entertainment within hotel or at nearby associate hotels.

🛏 123 🛁 84 G ↕ TV C ☎ ☕ ▥

ROYAL COURT—3-star hotel on sea front in own gardens directly opposite beach. Magnificent views.

🛏 56 🛁 34 G TV ☎ ▥ ⚲ ☕

ROSE AND CROWN—2-star hotel in own grounds close to town centre and beach. 'Victoriana' cocktail bar.

🛏 36 🛁 27 ↕ TV R ▥ ☕

CRAMOND HOUSE—2-star hotel in own grounds and centrally situated. Dancing within the hotel most Friday and Saturday evenings.

🛏 89 🛁 37 ↕ ☎ ▥ ⚲ ☕

BROWN'S—Central: A town centre hotel, in the same family ownership for 19 years. Wine served without extra charge at dinner.

🛏 30 ☕

WEST END—A family-owned hotel situated in own grounds convenient for shops and sea front. Early morning tea without additional charge.

🛏 54 🛁 20 G R

Checking information

Checking information
Can I (just) check (that) . . .?
Am I right in thinking that . . .?
I'd like to make sure (that) . . .
There *is* . . ., isn't there?
You *do* . . ., don't you?
I assume . . .
I take it . . .

Practice A [telephone conversation]
The Ship Inn. Can I help you?
I'd like to book two double rooms. **Am I right in thinking** you have a games room?
That's quite correct, sir..

The George Hotel. Can I help you?
I'd like to book a single room. **Can I just check that** there is TV in the bedrooms?
I'm sorry, sir. We haven't got TV in the bedrooms, but there *is* a TV lounge.

Practice B
You've stayed at the Regent's Palace, haven't you? **There** *is* a hairdressing salon, **isn't there?**
Yes, there is. There's a sauna too.

You've stayed at the Royal Court, haven't you? **I'd like to make sure that** it's in the centre of town.
No, it isn't, but it's opposite the beach.

Practice C
Am I right in thinking that the George is very expensive?
Well, it says it's a four-star hotel, if that's what you mean.

I take it the Rose and Crown is central.
Well, it says it's near the town centre, if that's what you mean.

FORMER JOBS OF FAMOUS PEOPLE

1	Sean Connery, actor	bricklayer
2	Albert Einstein, physicist	patent officer clerk
3	Gerald R Ford, president	male model
4	Clark Gable, actor	lumberjack
5	Guiseppe Garibaldi, revolutionary	sailor
6	Paul Gauguin, painter	stockbroker
7	Adolf Hitler, dictator	poster artist
8	Bob Hope, comedian	boxer
9	Marilyn Monroe, actress	factory worker
10	Elvis Presley, singer	truck driver

GERALD FORD

10 BIGGEST BEER-DRINKING COUNTRIES

		Litres per Capita
1	Czechoslovakia	152.7
2	West Germany	147
3	Australia	141.3
4	Belgium	140
5	Luxembourg	135
6	New Zealand	126.1
7	East Germany	114.9
8	United Kingdom	114.3
9	Denmark	111.96
10	Austria	106.2

20 NATIONS THAT CAN BLOW UP THE WORLD

1 People's Republic of China
2 France
3 India
4 United Kingdom
5 U.S.S.R.
6 U.S.A.
7 Canada
8 Republic of China (Taiwan)
9 Israel
10 Italy
11 Japan
12 South Africa
13 Spain
14 Sweden
15 Switzerland
16 Argentina
17 Austria
18 Belgium
19 Brazil
20 Czechoslovakia

A-bomb over Nagasaki. This explosion on August 9 1945 killed 74,800 people.

Reactions to information

Drawing attention to information
Do/Did you realize/know (that) . . .?
Listen to this!/According to . . .,/Apparently, . . .

Reacting with surprise
Goodness! I never knew that. (That *does* surprise me.)
He wasn't (, was he?)/They don't (, do they?) etc.
Fancy that!/Good heavens!
You must be joking/You're not serious, are you?

Dismissing
I can't believe there's any truth in that.
That can't be true/right.
Come off it!
So what?/Yes, I knew that.

Reacting with interest
Really?
How/That's interesting!

Reacting with horror
Oh no! How/That's awful/dreadful!
That doesn't bear thinking about.

Practice A
Did you know that Sean Connery, the actor, used to be a bricklayer?
Goodness, that *does* **surprise me.**

According to this list, Bob Hope, the comedian, used to be a boxer.
Yes, I knew that.

Practice B
Did you realize they drink more beer in Belgium than in Denmark?
They don't, do they?

Listen to this! They drink more beer in Luxembourg than in Austria.
That's interesting.

Practice C
Did you know that Switzerland can now blow up the world?
How awful!

Do you realize that India can now blow up the world?
You're not serious, are you?

JULY

1	Sun	**17**	Tues	*Lucy's driving test*
2	Mon	**18**	Wed	
3	Tues	**19**	Thurs	
4	Wed	**20**	Fri	
5	Thurs	**21**	Sat	*Tony and Joan getting married*
6	Fri	*Jack arriving*	**22**	Sun
7	Sat	**23**	Mon	
8	Sun	**24**	Tues	
9	Mon	**25**	Wed	
10	Tues	*Jack leaving*	**26**	Thurs — Ramadan starts
11	Wed	**27**	Fri	
12	Thurs	**28**	Sat	*Mary going on holiday*
13	Fri	*Bob and Ian's party*	**29**	Sun
14	Sat	**30**	Mon	*Browns' Silver Wedding anniversary*
15	Sun	**31**	Tues	
16	Mon			

Agreeing with and correcting statements of fact

Agreeing with a statement
(Yes,) that's right.
Yes (it is/they are).
I think/believe so.
As far as I know.

Correcting a statement
(No.) . . ., actually.
It doesn't/They aren't, you know. . . .
I don't think so. . . .
Isn't it/Aren't they . . .?
I'm not sure (about that). I think . . . (, actually/though).
You may be right, but I think . . .
Are you sure? I thought . . .

Practice A
Jack's arriving on the sixth, isn't he?
That's right.

Lucy's taking her driving test on a Tuesday, isn't she?
I think so.

Practice B
So the third of July is a Monday.
A Tuesday, **actually.**

So Ramadan starts on Saturday 14th.
It doesn't, you know. It starts on Thursday 26th.

Practice C
Jack's leaving on Tuesday 10th.
As far as I know.

Mary's going on holiday on Saturday 14th.
Are you sure? I thought she was going on Saturday 28th.

The Political Weekly

This graph shows the rise and fall in the popularity of the government over the past year.

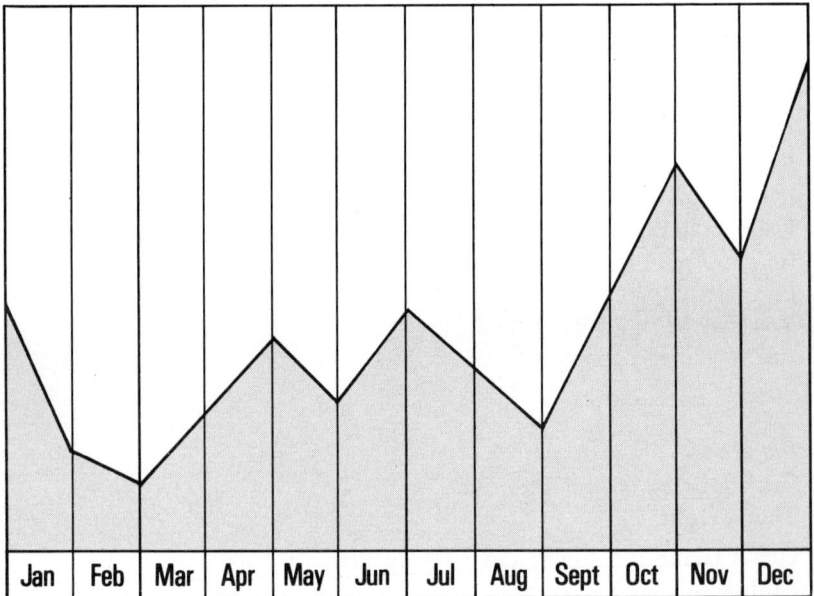

| Jan | Feb | Mar | Apr | May | Jun | Jul | Aug | Sept | Oct | Nov | Dec |

Jan   Introduction of petrol rationing
Feb   Devaluation of the pound
Mar   Acceptance of the IMF loan
Apr   Settlement of wage claims
May   Refusal to help farmers
Jun   Success in selling Concordes
Jul   Restrictions of imports
Aug   Closure of factories
Sept Prevention of dock strike
Oct   Expansion of trade with Europe
Nov   Decision to cut public services
Dec   Reduction in income tax

Explanations

Asking for an explanation
Why . . .?
What was the reason for . . .?
What was behind . . .?
What caused/led to . . .?
Can you explain . . .?
How do/would you account for . . .?

Giving an explanation
(. . .) because (of)/owing to/due to . . .
. . . and . . . as a result.
. . . which is why . . .
. . . as a result/with the result that/consequently . . .
. . . can be (directly) attributed to . . .
The reason for . . . is/was/has been . . .
It is/seems to be a (direct) result of . . .
I'd put it down to . . .

Not giving an explanation
It's beyond me/Goodness (only) knows!
I (really) don't know (why . . .).
(Well,) it's too complicated to go into now.

Practice A
Why were the Government so unpopular in January?
Because they introduced petrol rationing.

Can you explain the Government's popularity in March?
I'd put it down to their acceptance of an IMF loan.

Practice B
What was behind the rise in the Government's popularity in October?
Goodness only knows!

Why was there a decline in their popularity in May?
Well, it's too complicated to go into now.

Practice C
The Government lost a lot of support in July, didn't they?
Yes. They restricted imports, **which is why** they became less popular.

The Government gained a lot of support in June, didn't they?
Yes. They sold more Concordes and **consequently** became more popular.

Test of social attitudes

Tick one box each time. ☐

Adverts
Adverts are a waste of money. ☐
Adverts are interesting. ☐

Pollution
We should stop pollution. ☐
If we want industry, we must have pollution. ☐

The energy problem
There is plenty of energy for everyone. ☐
We should try to save energy. ☐

Women's rights
Women should have equal rights. ☐
A woman's place is in the home. ☐

Dealing with criminals
Criminals should go to prison. ☐
Criminals are sick people who need help. ☐

Smoking
We should ban cigarettes. ☐
People should be allowed to smoke. ☐

War
All war is wrong. ☐
Some wars are necessary. ☐

Nuclear weapons
It is wrong to make nuclear weapons. ☐
Without nuclear weapons there would be more wars. ☐

Animal experiments
We should ban experiments on animals. ☐
Animal experiments help humans. ☐

Opinions

Asking about opinions

What do you think/feel (about . . .)?
What's your opinion (on/about . . .)?
Do you have any views (on . . .)?
Do/Would you agree/think/say (that) . . . (or . . .)?
Wouldn't you say (that) . . .?
In your opinion, . . .?

Giving an opinion

I think/believe/feel (that) . . .
It's my belief/view/feeling/opinion (that) . . .
In my opinion/view . . .
It seems to me (that) . . .
As far as I can see/As I see it . . .
Surely . . .

Not giving an opinion

I don't feel strongly either way (in actual fact).
I don't know enough about it (to form an opinion) (, I'm afraid).
I can see both points of view (actually).
I really don't know (what I think) (about that/any more).
Who cares?

Practice A

What do you think about women's rights?
I believe women should have equal rights.

What's your opinion on nuclear weapons?
It seems to me that without nuclear weapons there would be more wars.

Practice B

Do you agree there is plenty of energy for everyone?
I don't know enough about it to form an opinion, I'm afraid.

Wouldn't you say that animal experiments help humans?
I really don't know what I think any more.

Practice C

In your opinion, are adverts interesting or a waste of time?
Surely they're a waste of time.

Do you think all war is wrong **or** some wars are necessary?
I can see both points of view actually.

National Party

- People ought to work more overtime
- The rich pay too much tax
- Strikes are usually the workers' fault
- There is very little poverty in our country
- We should sell more to Europe
- We need to spend more on industry
- Schools should teach facts
- The police have too little power

Social Party

- People ought to work less overtime.
- The rich pay too little tax
- Strikes are usually the management's fault
- Poverty is our worst problem
- We should sell more to the Third World
- We need to spend more on schools and hospitals
- Schools should help children think for themselves
- The police have too much power

Agreeing
(Yes,) I agree/I'd agree (with that/you).
I don't disagree (with that/you).
(That's) right.
(Yes,) of course/indeed.
Absolutely/I couldn't agree more/Quite.

Disagreeing
(I'm afraid) I disagree/don't agree/can't agree (with that/you).
I'm not (so) sure (about that).
I wouldn't say that (exactly).
Do you really think so?/You can't mean that.
(No,) I can't accept that.
No, I think . . .
(But) surely . . .?
Don't you think . . .?
Rubbish!/Come on!/Surely not!

Asking if someone agrees
I think . . . . Don't you?
. . . Don't you agree?

Practice A
It says here that schools should teach facts.
Well, **I agree with that.**

It says here that poverty is our worst problem.
Well, **I'm not so sure about that.**

Practice B
In my opinion we should sell more to Europe.
I agree with you. We *should* sell more to Europe.

I think the rich pay too little tax.
I wouldn't say that. I think they pay too *much* tax.

Practice C
I think we need to spend more on industry. **Don't you?**
Yes, indeed.

In my opinion people ought to work more overtime. **Don't you agree?**
No, I think people ought to work less overtime.

Miss World

The World Cup

The Eurovision Song Contest

The World Chess Championships

Predictions

Asking for predictions
What/Who (do you think) is going to/will/is most likely to . . .?
Do you think . . . or . . . will/is going to . . .?
Who/What would you put your money on to . . .?

Predicting
(I'm sure/certain that) . . . will/is going to . . .
. . . is bound/sure/certain/likely to (. . .) .
I expect/(should) think/bet/reckon (that) . . .will/is going to . . .
. . . might/may/could/must . . .
I'll stick my neck out and say . . .
It's got to be . . .
If . . . doesn't . . ., I'll eat my hat.
. . . stand a (good) chance (of . . .).
I'd put my money on . . .

Not predicting
I don't know/I have no idea. (I don't know much about . . .)
Goodness/God (only) knows!
It's anybody's guess.
Anybody/Anything could . . .
I wish I knew.
I don't think . . . will . . ., but I don't know who/what will.

Practice A
Who do you think will be the next Miss World?
I'll stick my neck out and say Miss Holland.

Who do you think will win the Eurovision Song Contest?
Goodness knows!

Practice B
If Russia **doesn't** win the world chess championships, **I'll eat my hat.**
Yes, they**'re bound to.**

I reckon Italy **are going to** win the World Cup.
Oh no! **It's got to be** Brazil.

Practice C
I don't think Greece **will** win, **but I don't know who will.**
France **stands a good chance.**

I don't think Miss Japan will win, **but I don't know who will.**
I'd put my money on Miss United States of America.

The man who
lived for ever

Travelling
Through
Time

The dinosaurs come back

Robots take over
the world

It's the end of
the world

The new ice age

War with Mars

The man who could
read people's thoughts

The last person
on earth

Imagination

Asking someone to imagine a situation
What if . . .?
(Just) imagine/I wonder what it would be like if . . .
(Just) suppose/supposing . . .
I wonder what it would be like if/to . . .
What would happen/What would you do/How would you feel if . . .
What do you think it would be like if/to . . .?
Can you imagine . . .?
Think of . . .

Imagining a situation
(If . . .,) . . . would/'d/wouldn't . . . (, wouldn't/would it?)
(I suppose/think) I'd/it'd . . .
I really don't know (what I'd do). (I suppose . . .)
I can't say. (I suppose . . .)
Who knows? Maybe/Perhaps I'd/it'd . . .
I/It might . . ., I suppose.

Practice A
Supposing you could read people's thoughts.
It'd be very interesting!
Just imagine what it would be like if robots took over the world.
It'd be awful, **wouldn't it!**

Practice B
What would you do if you were the last person on earth?
I can't say. Perhaps I'd like it.

What would you do if there was a new ice age?
Who knows? I might become an astronaut!

Practice C
If we could travel through time, **I'd** go back to the time of the Romans.
Would you? **I think I'd** go forward to the year 2,000.

If we lived for ever, **I'd** work in every country in the world.
Would you? **I think I would** too.

Practice D
It'd be frightening **if** the dinosaurs came back, **wouldn't it?**
Who knows? Maybe it'd be rather interesting.

It'd be fascinating to read other people's thoughts, **wouldn't it?**
Who knows? It might be rather embarrassing.

FILMS

ODEON ONE
Star Wars

ODEON TWO
Superman

PLAZA
Watership Down

ABC 1
The Deer Hunter

ABC 2
The Private Life of Sherlock Holmes

THEATRES

Playhouse
UNCLE VANYA
by Chekhov

Palace
HAMLET
by William Shakespeare

Little Theatre
A MURDER IS ANNOUNCED
by Agatha Christie

Grand
BEDROOM FARCE
by Alan Ayckbourn

OPERA

THE LOMBARDS
by Verdi
performed by
ALBION OPERA COMPANY
at
Royal Theatre

THE PEARL FISHERS
by Bizet
performed by
UNIVERSITY OPERA GROUP
at
University Main Hall

CONCERTS

at
Queens Hall
BBC SYMPHONY ORCHESTRA
perform
Weber Overture
Oberon
Mozart Piano Concerto No 24
and
Beethoven Symphony No 3

---

at
St Georges Hall
ROYAL ORCHESTRA
perform
Mozart Symphony No 38
Liszt Piano Concerto No 1
and
Stravinsky Petruska

JAZZ CLUBS

New Orleans Club
Modern Jazz Club

FOLK CLUBS

White Swan Folk Club
Pack Horse Folk Club
Real Ale Folk Club

EXHIBITIONS AND MARKETS

Westminster Gallery (abstracts)
Goosewell Gallery (landscapes)
Antique and Collectors' Fair

NIGHT CLUBS

The Entertainer
Disco-Club

RESTAURANTS

Chez Marcel
Oakwood House
Berkley
Curry-Indian

Decisions

Asking someone to make a decision
Do you want to . . .?
(What) are you going to . . .?
Have you decided/made up your mind (. . .)?

Making a decision
I've decided to/against . . .
I've made up my mind (not) to . . .
I'm doing . . .
I'm going to . . .
I know. I'll . . .
(Yes/No,) I think/don't think . . .

Not making a definite decision
I might (. . .).
I might do.
Perhaps/Maybe I'll . . .
I think I'll . . .

Not deciding
I don't know whether/what to . . .
I can't decide/make up my mind (what/whether . . .)
It's up to you/I'm easy.

Practice A
Do you want to see a film?
No, I don't think so.

Are you going to have a meal at a restaurant?
I might do.

Practice B
Have you decided what you're going to do?
I know. I'll go to the theatre.
Which play **do you want to** see?
Uncle Vanya.

Where **do you want to** go?
I think I'll go to a folk club.
Which one?
I can't make up my mind.

BRANFORD COLLEGE

PROGRAMME OF EVENING CLASSES

Mon-Fri   7.00-9.00

Mon

French (1st year); Spanish (2nd year);
Shorthand; Dressmaking; Painting;
Ballroom dancing; Golf

Tues

Economics; Spanish (1st year); German
(2nd year); French (3rd year); Yoga;
Sculpture; Photography; Badminton

Weds

Mathematics (1st year); French (2nd year);
Woodwork; Cake decorating; Dog training;
Bridge; Soccer

Thurs

Biology; Mathematics (2nd year); German
(1st year); Car maintenance; Gardening;
Cookery; Singing; Keep fit

Fri

Sociology; Geology; German (3rd year);
Typing; Flower arranging; Pottery;
Guitar playing; Rugby; Swimming

Intentions

Asking about intentions
Are you going to . . .?
Do you intend to . . .?
Will you be doing . . .?

Expressing an intention
I'm going to (. . .)
I intend to (. . .)
I'll be doing . . .
I mean to (. . .)
I've decided to (. . .)
I might (well) (. . .)
I'm thinking of . . .

Changing your mind
I was going to . . . but . . . (instead).

Practice A
Are you going to go to any classes on Tuesdays?
Yes, **I'm going to** do yoga.

Do you intend to go to any classes on Fridays?
No, not on Fridays.

Practice B
Do you intend to take classes in woodwork?
Yes, **I mean to.**

Will you be taking classes in geology?
Well, **I'm thinking of** doing so.

Practice C
Are you going to do cookery on Thursdays?
I was going to, but I've decided to do gardening **instead.**

Are you going to do shorthand on Mondays?
I was going to, but I mean to do French **instead.**

USA TOURS

Visit a National Park.
Stay on a ranch.
See Disneyland.

Barbados
Go on a cruise.
Listen to calypsos.
Enjoy the sunshine.

Italy
See Pompeii.
Visit famous art galleries.
Enjoy the food.

England
Visit Shakespeare's house.
Explore the countryside.
Go shopping in London.

Egypt
Tour historic places.
Visit the pyramids.
See the treasures of Tutankhamun.

France
Drink lots of wine.
Enjoy the night life of Paris.
Visit old chateaux.

Switzerland
Go skiing.
See the lakes.
Explore the mountains.

Kenya
Go on safari.
Go fishing.
Relax in the sun.

Plans

Asking about plans
Are you doing . . .?
Are you going/planning to . . .?
Do you plan to . . .?
What are you doing . . .?
What are your plans (for . . .)?
Have you got anything on/planned/fixed (up) (for . . .)?

Describing plans
I'm/She's visiting/touring . . . etc.
I'm going/planning to . . .
I plan to . . .
I've arranged/fixed up to . . .
I've got something on/arranged/fixed (up) (for . . .)

Having no plans
I have/'ve got no plans.
I don't have/haven't got any plans.
I'm leaving it open/to chance.
(I was going/planning to . . ., but) everything's fallen through.

Practice A
Where **are you going** for your holiday?
I plan to go to France.

What **are you doing** for your holiday?
We were going to go to Russia, **but everything's fallen through.**

Practice B
Do you know anyone who**'s going** to Italy?
Anna **is going** there in July.

Do you know anyone who**'s going** to the USA?
No, I don't know anyone who**'s planning to** go there.

Practice C
What **are you going to do** in the USA?
I'm going to stay on a ranch, but otherwise **I don't have any plans.**

What **do you plan** to do in Italy?
I'm planning to visit famous art galleries, but otherwise **I'm leaving it open.**

Duty-free list

Spirits and wines are sold by the litre or half-litre.
Cigarettes are normally sold in packs of 100 or 200 but
packets of 20 may sometimes be available.
Perfume is available in quarter- or half- ounce bottles.

Whisky
   Vat 69
   Teacher's
   Johnny Walker

Brandy
   Martell Four Star
   Courvoisier
   Napoleon

Gin
   Gordon's
   Booth's
   Beefeater

Liqueurs
   Drambuie
   Cointreau
   Chartreuse

Fortified Wines
   Sherry
   Port

Cigarettes
   Benson and Hedges
   Dunhill
   Lucky Strike

Perfumes
   Worth—Je Reviens
   Chanel No. 5
   Carven—Ma Griffe

Requests for things

Saying what you want
A(n) packet/bottle/half bottle of . . . please.
A(n) litre/pound/ounce of . . . please.
Half a litre/pound/ounce of . . . please.
Ten/Two hundred . . . please.
I'd like . . . please.
Can I have . . .?
Have you got any . . . (for under/about £ . . .)?
I'll take the . . ./that then.

Changing your mind
(Sorry,) could I change that to . . .?
(Sorry,) can we make that . . .?
(Sorry,) I think I'll leave it (after all) (, thank you).

Practice A
Two hundred Dunhill **please.**
Here you are, sir.
Thank you.

Half an ounce of Ma Griffe **please.**
Here you are, madam.
Thank you.

Practice B
I'd like a bottle of Chartreuse **please.**
I'm sorry, we've sold out. We've got Drambuie or Cointreau.
Oh no. **I think I'll leave it, thank you.**

A half bottle of Martell **please.**
I'm sorry, we've only got full bottles.
I'll take that then.

Practice C
Half an ounce of Je Reviens **please.**
Certainly, sir.
Sorry, can we make that an ounce?
Yes, sir.

Can I have two hundred Lucky Strike **please.**
Certainly, madam.
Sorry. Could I change that to Benson and Hedges?
Yes, madam.

SHOPPING

1 lb mince
6 oranges
1 brown loaf
red wine
milk
aspirins
New York Times

N.B.

Return library books
Collect suit from dry-cleaners
Make hair appointment for 10 a.m., Sat.
Book 2 theatre tickets for Sat. night
Post parcel

Requests to do things

Making a request
Would/Could you do me a favour?
Can I ask you to do me a favour?
Do you think you could . . . for me?
I'd be (very) grateful if you could/would/wouldn't mind . . . (for me).
(If you're . . .,) can/could/would you . . . (for me)?
(If you're . . .,) would you mind . . . (for me)?
Can/Could/Would you get/buy (me) . . .?
Would you mind getting/buying (me) . . .?
Are you/Will you be . . . (by any chance)?

Agreeing to a request
No problem!
(Yes,) of course/certainly/willingly/all right/OK/sure.

Agreeing reluctantly to a request
(Well,) I suppose so.
(Well,) I'll try, but I can't promise (anything).
(Well,) it's a bit difficult/awkward (as/because . . .), but I will if you can't find anyone else (to).

Refusing a request
Any other time (but . . .).
I'm afraid I can't/haven't much time today . . .
I'm (terribly/so) sorry, but . . .
Well, it's a bit/rather awkward/difficult (actually/I'm afraid).

Practice A
Are you going past the butcher's? **Could you** buy a pound of mince **for me?**
Yes, OK.

Will you be going to the supermarket? **Would you mind getting me** a pint of milk?
I'm terribly sorry, but I'm not going that way.

Practice B
Would you do me a favour? D'you think you could return this library book **for me?**
Certainly.

Can I ask you to do me a favour? I'd be grateful if you'd book two theatre tickets for Saturday night **for me.**
Well, I'm afraid I haven't much time today.

For Reference Only

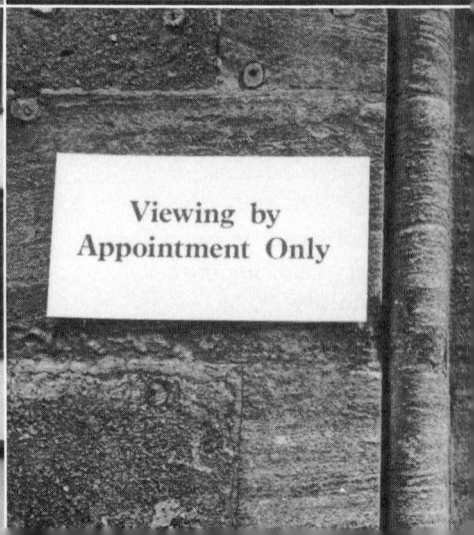

OXFORD · OXFORD · OXFORD · OXF

VOLUME I VOLUME II
A-E F-K

NO CAMPING WITHOUT PERMISSION

PLEASE KEEP OFF THE GRASS

Please do not touch

Except for access

Viewing by Appointment Only

Permission

Asking permission
Can/May I . . .?
Would you mind/Would it be all right if I . . .?
Is it all right/OK to . . .?
Am I allowed to . . .?
Is there any chance of my . . .?

Giving permission
(Yes,) go ahead/all right/certainly.
Of course (you can/may/are).
By all means.
I suppose so (, just this once). [*reluctant*]
If you must/want. [*reluctant*]

Refusing to give permission
I'm sorry,/I'm afraid you mustn't/can't/aren't allowed to . . .
(I'm afraid) I can't let you . . .
(It's OK with me, but) you'd better ask . . .
(It's) out of the question (, I'm afraid).

Practice A
I'm afraid you aren't allowed to take those books out of the library.
Oh, I'm sorry. I didn't realize.

I'm sorry, you aren't allowed on the grass.
Oh, I'm sorry. I didn't realize.

Practice B
Would it be all right if I camped here for the night?
By all means.

May we look round the house?
Yes, certainly.

Practice C
Is there any chance of my driving down there?
Out of the question, I'm afraid.

Is it all right to walk on the grass?
I suppose so, just this once.

Hanson's Mail Order Catalogue

Do your Christmas shopping the easy way. Choose
your gifts in the comfort of your own home.

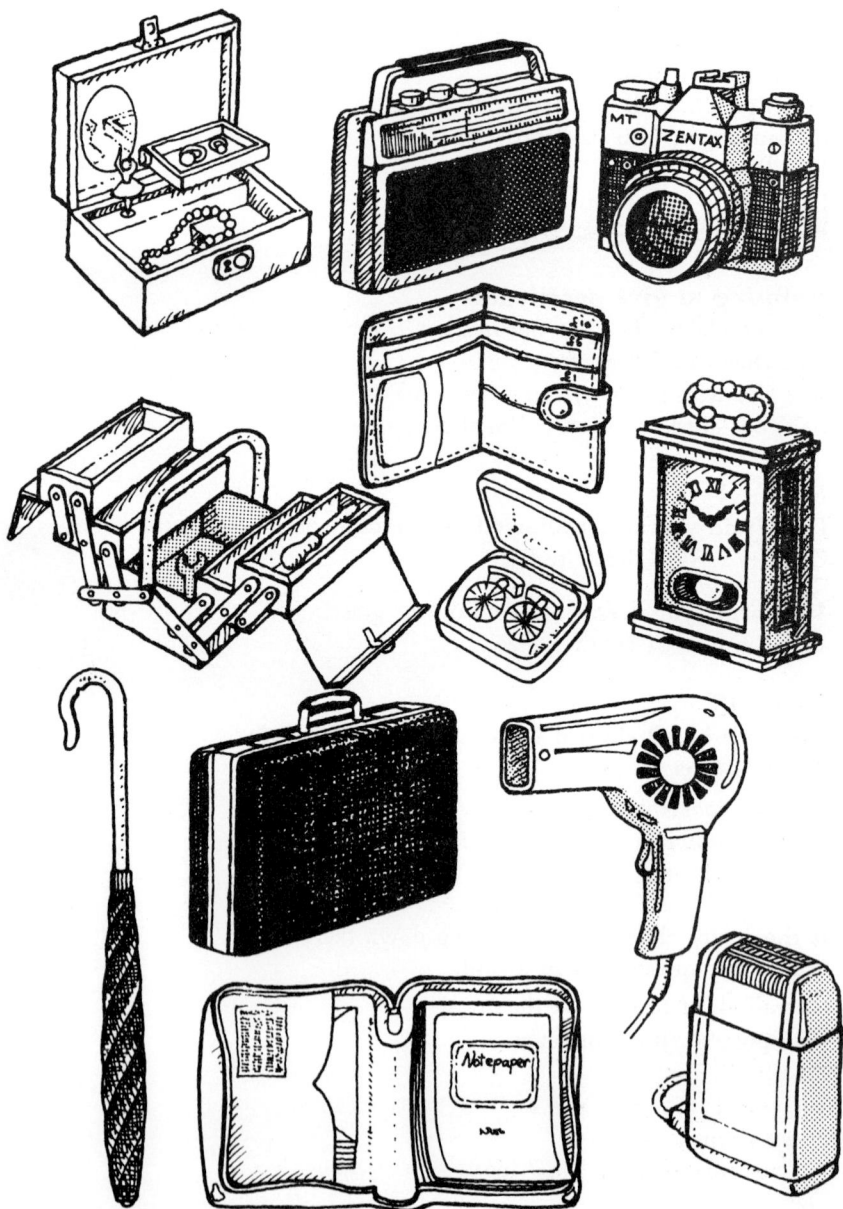

Suggestions

Asking for suggestions
. . . shall/should/can . . .?
Have you (got) any idea/suggestions . . .?
Can you suggest . . .?
What (on earth) . . .?

Making suggestions
What/How about . . .?
Why don't/not . . .?
Let's . . . (, shall we?)
Shall/Should/Couldn't . . .?

Agreeing with a suggestion
(Yes,) all right/OK.
(Yes.) Let's (do that).
(That's a) good idea/suggestion.
What a good/splendid/clever idea!
Why not?

Disagreeing with a suggestion
I'm not (so) sure/I don't think that's a good idea.
(No,) let's . . . (instead).
Don't let's . . .
(Oh no,) not again!

Practice A
What **shall** we give your mother for Christmas?
How about getting her a hair-dryer?
No, **I don't think that's a good idea.**

Have you any idea what we should get for Tom?
Why don't we give him a pair of cuff-links?
Yes, let's do that.

Practice B
Who **shall** we give the radio to?
Couldn't we give it to Tom?
Oh yes! **Why not?**

Who **can** I give the wallet to?
What about Julie?
I'm not sure that's a good idea.

The 'Consumer's Guide' Report on Washing-Machines.

	How big?	How reliable?	How cheap?
Superclean	••	•••	•••••
Washermatic	•	••	••
Dynawhite	•••	•	••••
Maxiwash	•••	••••	••
Cleaneasy	•	•••	•••
Luxomat	••	••	•
Powerex	•••	•	••
Homewash	••	••	•••
Washerette	••	•	••••
Autowash	•	••	••••

••• large	•••• very reliable	••••• very cheap
•• medium	••• good	•••• quite cheap
• small	•• quite reliable	••• medium priced
	• not very reliable	•• quite expensive
		• very expensive

Advice

Asking for advice
Would you advise me to . . .?
Would you . . . (if you were me)?
What do you think I should/ought to . . .?
What/Which (. . .) should I . . .?
Can you advise me . . .?
Can you give me any advice on/about . . .?
I'm thinking of . . .

Giving advice
You should/shouldn't . . .
You ought (not) to . . . (, then).
You'd better (not) . . .
I would/wouldn't/should/shouldn't . . . (if I were you).
I'd advise you (not) to . . .
If you take my advice, you'll/you won't . . .

Practice A
I want a small washing-machine.
You ought to get a Washermatic **then.**

I want a medium-priced washing-machine.
I would get a Cleaneasy, **if I were you.**

Practice B
Which washing machine **should I** get? A Superclean or a Washermatic?
You'd better get a Superclean. It's more reliable.

Can you advise me which washing-machine to get? A Dynawhite or a Maxiwash?
I'd advise you to get a Dynawhite. It's cheaper.

Practice C
I'm thinking of buying an Autowash.
I'd advise you not to. It's very small.

I'm thinking of buying a Washerette.
I wouldn't, if I were you. It's not very reliable.

The Gourmet's Guide to Inexpensive Eating in London

CENTRAL LONDON

Sharaton Pâtisserie

teashop specializing in cakes and pastries

270 Edgeware Road

Open 0830-1800
Closed Sun & Bank Holidays
Salami & pickle roll 32p
Apple strudel 29p

CITY

Slenders Health Food

specializes in vegetarian food

14 Cannon Street

Open 0830-1815
Closed Sat, Sun & Bank Holidays
Spinach, egg & cheese flan 65p
Mixed fruit crumble 38p
PNCP near St Paul's WC

HAMPSTEAD

Viva Tacos

Specializes in Mexican food

25 Belsize Park

Open 1100-0100 (Sun till 2400)
Taco 34p Burrito 44p
P side streets around

PICCADILLY

Stockpot

specializes in omelettes and quiches

4 Haymarket

Open 1200-2200 (Sun till 2000)
Closed Easter Sunday, 25 & 26 December
Spanish omelette 50p
Spinach quiche & salad 65p
P in nearby side street WC

SOHO

Village Chinese Restaurant

specializes in Chinese food

16 Charing Cross Rd.

Open 1200-1800
Closed 25 December
Dim sum 35p Cheung fan 45p
P St Anne's Church car park in Dean St WC

Shampers

specializes in cold dishes

40 Hanover Square

Open 1100-1500 & 1730-2300, Sat 1100-1500
Closed Sun & Bank Holidays
Cold pork & barbecue sauce 90p
Smoked mackerel mousse 70p
PNCP opposite WC

VICTORIA

La Tavola Calda

specializes in Italian food

31 Buckingham Gate

Open 1200-2300
Closed Sun & Bank Holidays
Spaghetti 85p Lasagne 95p
P surrounding streets WC

Seafresh

specializes in traditional English fish and chips

108 Vauxhall Bridge

Open 1200-1500 & 1700-2300, Sat 1200-2300
Closed Sun
Haddock & chips £1.15
Chicken salad £1.20
P streets WC

Recommendations

Asking for a recommendation
Can you recommend (a good) . . .?
Do you know of a good . . .?
Is . . . any good (, do you know)?
Would you recommend . . .?

Giving a recommendation
Try . . . . It's excellent/very good/rather good/first rate.
I like . . . (myself).
(If you like . . .,) . . . is excellent/very good.
I (would/can/thoroughly) recommend . . .

Not giving a recommendation.
I wouldn't recommend . . .
(No,) . . . isn't up to much.
I was (very) disappointed by it, actually.

Practice A
Can you recommend a restaurant that serves fish and chips?
Try Seafresh, in Victoria. **It's rather good.**

Do you know of a good vegetarian restaurant?
I can recommend Slenders Health Food.

Practice B
Can you recommend a restaurant in Piccadilly?
The Stockpot **is very good. I like** their quiche.

Is the fish and chip restaurant in Victoria **any good?**
No, it isn't up to much, but the Italian restaurant there **is excellent.**

Practice C
Do you know of a good vegetarian restaurant?
I thoroughly recommend Slenders Health Food in the City.
Can you park near there?
There's a car park near St Paul's.

Can you recommend a good restaurant in the Hampstead area?
Viva Tacos is excellent.
Is it very expensive?
Well, you can get burrito for 44p.

Reminders

Reminding
Don't forget (to) . . . (,will you?)
Make sure you . . (, won't you?)
Be sure to . . .
Remember (to) . . . (, won't you?)
Have you (remembered to) . . .?
You'll/You will . . ., won't you?
You won't forget (to) . . ., will you?

Responding to reminders
I will/won't.
Of course (I will/I won't/not).
Thank goodness you've reminded me.
It's a good thing you said that. I'd have forgotten all about it
(otherwise).

Practice A
I'm off on holiday the day after tomorrow.
Lucky you! **Don't forget to** cancel the milk, **will you?**

I'm off on holiday the day after tomorrow.
Lucky you! **Have you** asked someone to feed the cat?

Practice B
Right, we're off.
Have you left a light on?
Thank goodness you've reminded me! I'll go and turn one on now.

Right, we're off.
Be sure to lock the doors and windows, **won't you?**
Of course! I'll go and lock them now.

Practice C
Where are you?
I'm just turning off the electricity.
Remember to turn off the gas too, **won't you?**
I will.

Where are you going?
I'm just going to ask the neighbours to watch the house.
You will ask them to feed the cat too, **won't you?**
I will.

CAUTION
This substance is caustic. It can cause burns. Close the lid firmly after use.

BEWARE OF THE DOG.

POISON
This liquid is highly poisonous. It can kill. Keep under lock and k

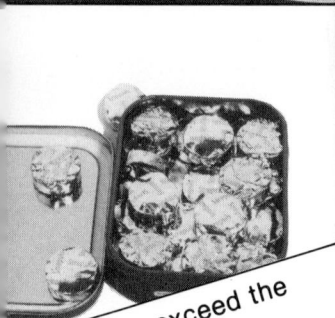

Do not exceed the stated dose.

WARNING
Plastic bags can be dangerous. To avoid danger of suffocation keep this bag away from babies and children.

DANGER. HIGH VOLTAGE.

WARNING
Dangerous tides. Swimmers can be carried out to sea.

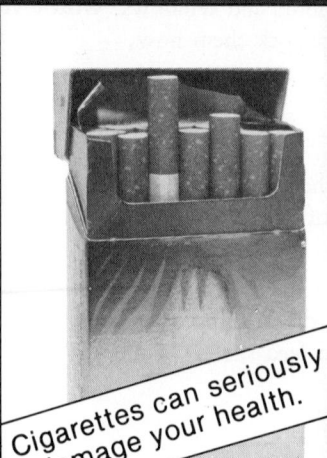

Cigarettes can seriously damage your health.

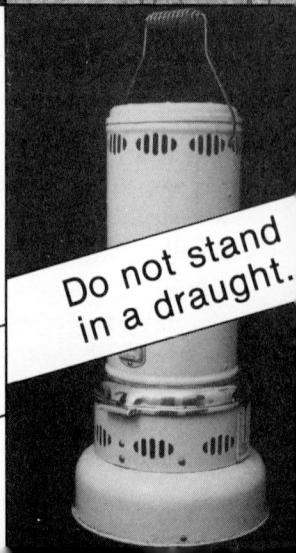

Do not stand in a draught.

Warnings

Warning
You shouldn't/ought not to . . . (, you know).
I should/shouldn't/would/wouldn't . . . (if I were you).
Be careful (not) to/you don't . . .
Be careful with . . . .
It'd be very silly/risky to . . .
Don't/you mustn't . . . (in case) . . .

Accepting a warning
True/OK/Thanks.
You're right.
Thank goodness you said/mentioned that.
Yes, I know (. . .).

Rejecting a warning
Rubbish/Nonsense!
There's nothing to worry about.
Don't fuss!
Why (not)?

Practice A
You ought not to smoke cigarettes, **you know.**
Yes, I know they can damage your health.

Be careful with the substance in that tin.
Yes, I know it can cause burns.

Practice B
Don't leave that bottle there!
Why not?
In case someone poisons themselves.
Thank goodness you mentioned that.

You mustn't bathe here.
Why not?
In case you're carried out to sea.
Oh, **don't fuss!**

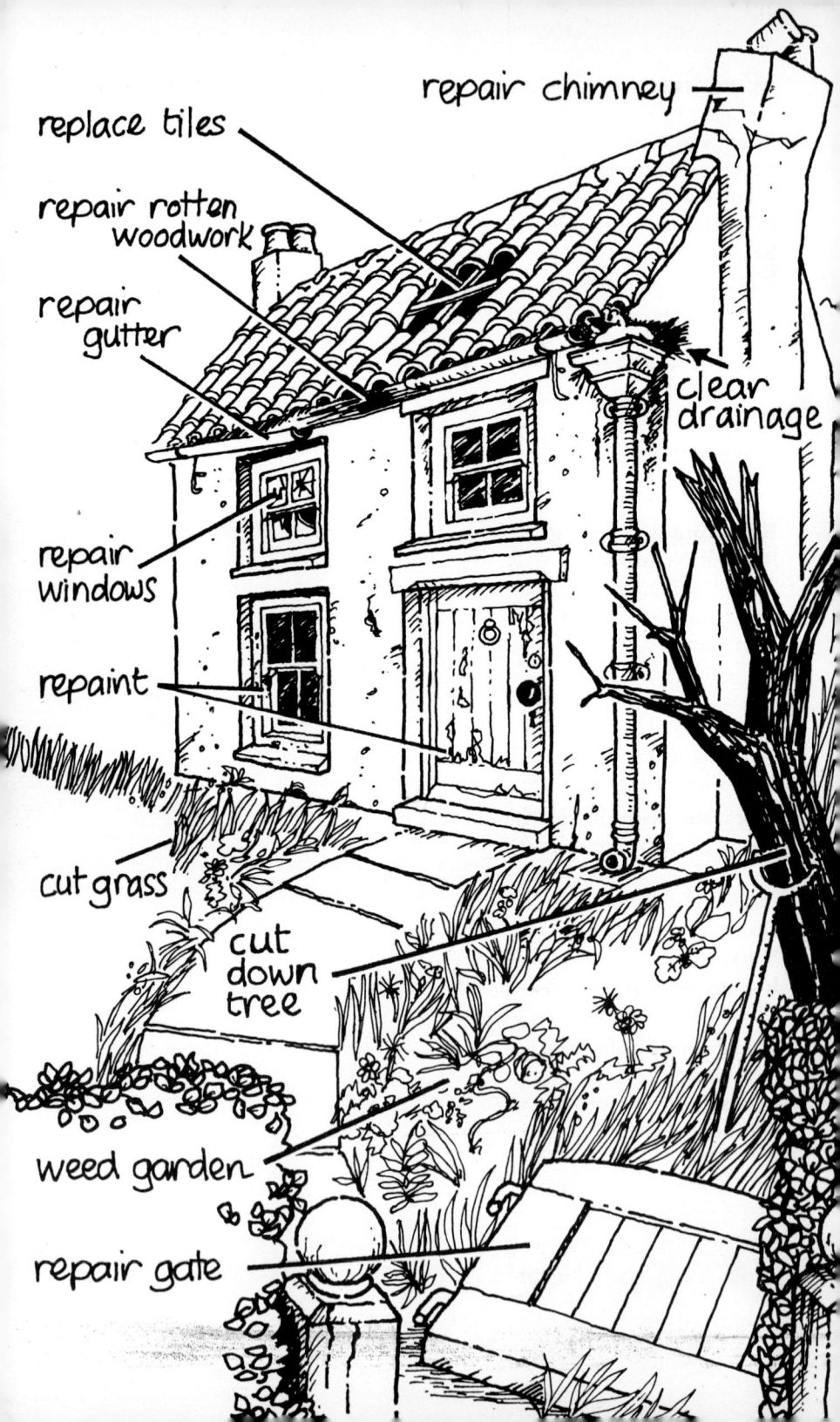

repair chimney

replace tiles

repair rotten
woodwork

repair
gutter

clear
drainage

repair
windows

repaint

cut grass

cut
down
tree

weed garden

repair gate

Insistence, threats and promises

Insisting
You (simply/really) must . . . (, you know).
You must . . . without fail/delay.
I insist that you . . .
I insist on your doing/. . .
It's imperative/essential (that) . . .

Threatening
If you (don't) . . ., I will/won't . . .
If you . . ., you'll be sorry.
. . . or else (. . .).
I won't . . . unless/until . . .

Promising
I promise (I will/won't . . .).
I will/shall/won't . . . (, I promise/honestly).
I will/won't, I promise you.
I give you my word (I'll . . .).
You can count on me.
Leave it with me.

Practice A
You really must do something about those tiles, **you know.**
I'll replace them, **I promise.**

It's essential that you cut down that tree.
Leave it with me.

Practice B
If you don't do something about those windows, **I won't** pay my rent.
Leave it with me.

I won't spend another night in the house **unless** you do something about that chimney.
I give you my word I'll ring the builder tomorrow.

Practice C
I'll see the tiles are replaced as soon as possible.
You do that **or else!**

I'll see the garden is weeded as soon as possible.
If you don't, **you'll be sorry.**

SOCIAL EVENTS IN BOXHILL THIS WEEK

Monday

Rotary Club Lunch - the Marine Hotel.
Guest Speaker - Mr David Bell.
Members and guests only.

Tuesday

Public Meeting in the Town Hall at 8 p.m.
to discuss the new Community Centre.

Wednesday

Women's Institute Coffee Morning at 11 a.m.
in St. Martin's Church Hall.

"Romeo and Juliet" - Shakespeare Touring Company.
One Performance Only - 7.45 p.m. at the King's Theatre.

Thursday

H. & W. Goodfellow Ltd. are holding a reception to
celebrate the 100th anniversary of the founding of
the Company. (by Invitation Only)

Friday

Exhibition of paintings by Ben Moore at the Castle
Gallery. Open all day.

Saturday

Football Match - Boxhill Rovers v. Hedley United.
Kick-off at 3 p.m. at Boxhill Park.

Disco at David Scott's club from 9 p.m. onwards.

Sunday

Morning Service at St. Martin's at 11 a.m.

Invitations

Inviting

Would you like to . . .?
(Do) come to . . .
Do you want to . . .?
I'd like to invite you to . . .
May I invite you to . . .?
Are you free/doing anything . . .?

Accepting an invitation

Yes, please.
(Thanks/Thank you/That's very kind of you.) (Yes,) I'd like/love to.
That would be very nice.
I'd be delighted to (. . .).
How nice/kind of you!
I'd be pleased/happy to (accept/ . . .).

Refusing an invitation

(That would be nice, but) I'm afraid . . .
(I'd love to, but) I'm afraid I can't.
Oh dear, what a pity! I . . .
(Sorry.) I'm afraid I have something else on/fixed up (. . .).

Practice A

Would you like to come to a coffee morning on Wednesday?
That would be very nice.

Do come to the disco on Saturday night.
I'd love to but I'm afraid I can't.

Practice B

The Shakespeare Touring Company are performing 'Romeo and Juliet' at the King's Theatre on Wednesday night. **Would you like to** come with me?
Thank you, I'd be delighted to.

Boxhill Rovers are playing Hedley United at Boxhill Park on Saturday afternoon. **D'you want to** come with us?
Yes, please.

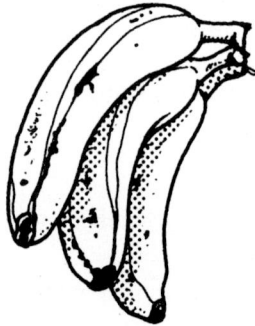

Offers of food and drink

Offering food and drink
Would you like . . .?
Can I get you anything/something (to eat/drink)?
Can I get/give you . . .?
Do you want . . .?
Have . . .
A/An/Some/A piece of/Some more/Another . . .?

Accepting an offer of food or drink
Thank you (very much).
(Yes.) Thanks. I'd love one/some.
(Yes.) Thanks. That would be nice.
Yes, please.
Well, if it's not too much trouble/if you're making some, . . .

Refusing an offer of food or drink
No/Not for me, thanks./thank you.
Not just at the moment, thanks/thank you/thanks all the same.
(It was/looks delicious, but) I'm afraid I couldn't.
I'm afraid I don't eat/drink . . .
I've had enough/plenty, thank you.
I'm afraid I'm not very fond of . . .

Practice A
Would you like a drink?
Thanks, I'd love one.

Do you want a biscuit?
That would be nice.

Practice B
Have another beer.
Not for me, thanks.

Can I give you some more cheese?
Yes, please.

Practice C
Can I get you something to drink?
Well, if it's not too much trouble.
A beer?
Yes, please.

OFFICE XMAS PARTY

on Saturday, 23 December

There will be a meeting in the Canteen on 10 December
to plan the Office Christmas Party for staff and their
friends. Everyone coming to the party should attend.

VOLUNTEERS will be required to bring

> Food
> Drink
> Records

We will also need VOLUNTEERS on Friday, 22 December to:

> fetch the Christmas tree
> put up the decorations
> shift the office furniture
> decorate the tree

... and during the party we will need VOLUNTEERS to:

> serve drinks at the bar
> look after the music
> organise the party games
> hand round the food

... and afterwards VOLUNTEERS will be needed to:

> wash up
> tidy up the office
> replace the furniture
> take back the empties

VOLUNTEER and make this year's party a great success.

Offers of help

Offering help
I'll . . . (, shall I?)
Shall/Can I . . . for you?
Would you like me to . . .?
Let me (. . .).
Is there anything I can do (to help)?

Accepting help
(Yes) please.
I'd appreciate it (if you could/would).
I'd be glad if you could/would.
(Thanks/Thank you.) That would be a great help.
That's very kind of you.
Could/Would you?

Refusing help
Thanks, but I can manage.
That's/I'm OK, thank you.
Don't worry/bother.
I'd rather/I'd better do it myself, thanks.
It's kind of you to offer, but . . .

Practice A
We'll need plenty of food.
I'll bake a cake, **shall I?**

We'll need plenty of drink.
Can I bring some beer?

Practice B
Shall I fetch the Christmas tree **for you?**
I'd better fetch it myself, thanks.

Let me wash up.
That's very kind of you.

£850

£260

£650

£725

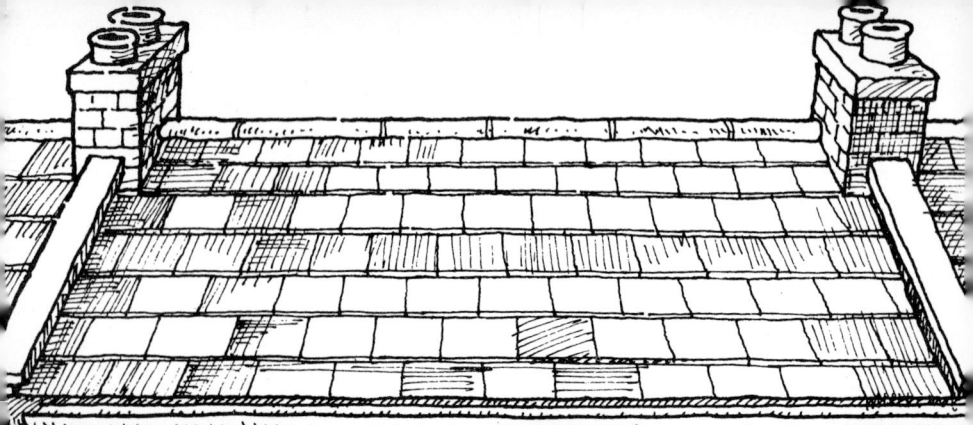

CARTER & WRIGHT LTD
electrical goods

£890

£950

£400

£190

£230

Refusals

Refusing gently
I must say/admit, I'm (rather/very) reluctant to (. . .).
That's rather . . ., isn't it?
Don't you think . . .?
Yes, but . . .
I can't see myself doing/. . .

Refusing
(I'm afraid/No) I won't/can't/I am not going to/ . . .).
(I'm afraid/No) that (just) isn't on.
(That's) out of the question (I'm afraid).

Refusing strongly
I will *not*. . .
I absolutely/simply refuse to . . .
There's no way I'm going to . . .
No way (will I/am I going to . . .)!
You must be joking!
Over my dead body!
Do you honestly think I . . .?
Who do you think I am?
If you think I'll . . ., you're wrong!

Practice A
That washing machine looks good.
Well, **I must admit I'm rather reluctant to** pay £725.

What about a colour television?
That's rather extravagant, **isn't it?**

Practice B
Are you sure you wouldn't like that vacuum cleaner?
Yes. **I'm not going to** pay £190.

Won't you think again about that washing machine?
No, **that's out of the question, I'm afraid.**

Practice C
You don't need a washing machine. You can wash everything by hand.
You must be joking!

You don't need a vacuum cleaner. You can use a dustpan and brush.
No way!

gate	flight	time	destination	
26	BA828	10 00	MELBOURNE	ON TIME
11	TW707	10 05	NEW YORK	3 HOURS DELAY
7	JL480	10 15	TOKYO	2 HOURS DELAY
22	BA291	10 20	MEXICO CITY	ON TIME
9	WT871	10 20	LAGOS	4 HOURS DELAY
6	AC358	10 25	VANCOUVER	ON TIME
20	IR755	10 30	TEHERAN	ON TIME
32	BA840	10 30	HONG KONG	3 HOURS DELAY
3	AC856	10 40	MONTREAL	2 HOURS DELAY
16	BA221	10 45	BERMUDA	6 HOURS DELAY
15	AI196	10 55	CALCUTTA	5 HOURS DELAY
34	BC659	11 00	RIO DE JANEIRO	ON TIME
25	BA012	11 00	NAIROBI	ON TIME
13	PA162	11 00	LOS ANGELES	ON TIME

Pleasure and Annoyance

Being pleased
Oh, I *am* pleased!
Oh, that *is* good (news)!
(Oh,/That's) good/fine/great/marvellous/excellent.
That's good to hear/know/see.

Being annoyed
Oh no/dear! (What a nuisance!)
(Oh,) damn/blast/hell/bloody hell! [*mild swear words*]
Would you believe it!
I don't believe it!
Just my luck!
I knew it!
Oh, that's (just) great/marvellous! [*sarcastic*]

Practice A
We are pleased to announce that Flight BA 828 to Melbourne will depart
on time.
Oh, good. We're going to be on time.
We are sorry to announce that Flight WT 871 to Lagos will depart four
hours late.
Oh, no! We're going to be four hours late. **What a nuisance!**

Practice B
I'm meeting someone on the flight from Vancouver.
Well, it's on time.
That's good.
I'm meeting someone on the flight from Calcutta.
Well, it's five hours late.
I don't believe it!

Practice C
Oh, hell!
What's the matter?
The flight to New York is three hours late.
Oh, that *is* **good news!**
You sound very cheerful.
I am. My flight to Melbourne is departing on time.

Come to Scotland

Likes and Dislikes

Likes
I like/enjoy/love . . .
I'm keen on/fond of . . .

Dislikes
I dislike/don't like/hate . . .
I'm not keen on/fond of . . .
I can't stand/bear . . .

Saying how much you like or dislike something
I love . . .
I like . . . very much./I'm very keen on . . .
I quite like . . . ./I'm quite keen on . . .
I don't like . . . very much./I'm not very keen on . . .
I don't like . . . at all./I'm not at all keen on . . .

Liking one thing more than another
I like . . . more/better than . . .
I prefer . . . (to . . .).
I like . . . best.
. . . is (not) my favourite (. . .).

Practice A
How about going sailing?
Yes, **I like** sailing.

How about a game of golf?
But **I don't like** golf.

Practice B
Do you like fishing?
Yes, I do. **I like** it **very much.**

Are you keen on walking?
No, I'm not. **I'm not at all keen on** it.

Practice C
Which do you like best, walking or riding?
I **like** riding **better than** walking.

Which do you prefer, golf or tennis?
I **prefer** tennis **to** golf.

BBC-1

5.05 **BLUE PETER** for children
5.40 **NEWS**
5.55 **NATIONWIDE** news reports
6.45 **TOMORROWS WORLD** new technology
7.35 **THE CIRCUS WORLD CHAMPIONSHIPS**
8.05 **KENNY ROGERS—IN CONCERT** America's country singer
9.00 **NINE O'CLOCK NEWS**
9.25 **THE GOOD OLD DAYS** Old time music hall
10.15 **TONIGHT** the stories behind the news
11.15 **SPORTSNIGHT** European football

BBC-2

4.50 **OPEN UNIVERSITY**
6.55 **TOP TABLE** International table-tennis
7.30 **NEWS**
7.40 **THE WORLD OF RUGBY**
8.05 **MAN ALIVE** documentary on an inner city area
9.00 **LIFE ON EARTH** nature series
9.50 **LOVE IN THE AFTERNOON** comedy film directed by Eric Rohmer
11.25 **LATE NEWS**
11.40 **ARENA: CINEMA** reports on films

ITV

5.05 **NEWS**
5.15 **CARTOON TIME**
5.30 **MUSIC** The Tom Robinson Band
6.00 **WHICKERS WORLD** travel programme
7.00 **QUESTION TIME** quiz programme
7.30 **THIS WEEK** current affairs
8.00 **FILM: CARNIVAL OF THIEVES** crime thriller
10.00 **NEWS**
10.30 **COLLISION COURSE** documentary about an air crash
11.00 **ONE FINE DAY** play by Alan Bennet

Preferences

Asking about preferences
Would you like/prefer (to) . . . or . . .?
Would you rather . . . or . . .?
Which/What would you prefer/like (to . . .)?
We can/could . . . or . . . (, whichever you like).
Do you want to . . . or . . .?

Expressing a preference
I'd prefer to . . . (, I must say).
I'd prefer . . . to . . . (, I must say).
I'd rather/sooner . . . (than . . .).
I feel more like . . . (myself).

Having no preference
I don't mind/care.
It's all the same to me.
It (really) doesn't matter to me.
It's up to you.
Whichever/Whatever you like.
You choose.
I'm easy.

Practice A
There's a film on ITV at eight o'clock, or **would you prefer** Kenny Rogers?
I'd rather watch the film **than** Kenny Rogers.

We could watch Sportsnight on BBC 1 at eleven fifteen, or there's a play on.
I feel more like the play **myself.**

Practice B
Do you want to watch the news **or** Sportsnight?
You choose.
Well, **I'd prefer to** watch the news, **I must say.**
Let's do that, then.

Would you rather watch table-tennis **or** a quiz programme?
Whichever you like.
Well, **I'd sooner** watch the table-tennis.
Let's do that, then.

Store Guide

Bathroom fittings	G		Lighting	3
Beds	3		Lingerie	2
Bicycles	3		Luggage	G
Books	G			
Boys' wear	1		Men's wear	1
Carpets	3		Paint	B
Children's wear	1		Perfumery	G
China	B		Photography	G
Clocks	G			
Cosmetics	G		Radio and television	3
Do-it-yourself	B		Scarves	G
			Sewing machines	1
Electrical appliances	B		Shoes	G
			Sports	3
Fashion fabrics	1		Stationery	G
Floorcoverings	3			
Food Hall	G		Tobaccos	1, G
Furniture and furnishings	3		Toilets (Men's)	1
			Toilets (Women's)	2
Gardening	B		Toiletries	G
Gifts	B		Toys	3
Girls' fashions	2		Typewriters	G
Glassware	B			
Gloves	G		Umbrellas	G
Greetings cards	G			
			Wallcoverings	B
Haberdashery	1		Watches	G
Handbags	G		Wine	G
Hardware	B		Wools	1
Hosiery	G		Women's fashions	2
Household linens	1			
Jewellery	G			

Wanting things

Saying what you want
I want/would like/need . . .
I want/would like/need to . . .
I'm looking for . . .
. . . please.

Asking what someone wants
What do you want (. . .)?
Is there anything you want?
Can I help you? [*shop assistant*]

Practice A
I need a clock.
Then you'll have to go to the ground floor. That's where the clocks are.

I want to buy some glasses.
Then you'll have to go to the basement. That's where the glassware is.

Practice B
I want to go to the basement.
So do I. **I want** to buy some china.
Oh, do you?

I need to go to the ground floor.
I do, too. **I want** some food.
So do I.

Practice C
What do you want to buy?
Some glasses.
Oh, glasses are in the basement.

Can I help you?
Yes please. **I'm looking for** a radio.
Oh, radios are on the third floor.

Wishes

Wishing to do things
I'd like to . . .
I'd love to . . .
I've always wanted to . . .
I've (often) dreamed of . . .
Haven't you always wanted to/dreamed of . . .?

Wishing to do things that you cannot do
I wish . . .
If only . . .
Wouldn't it be lovely to/if . . .

Practice A
Have you ever been to Turkey?
Yes, and **I'd like to** go there again some time.

Have you ever been to Iceland?
No, but **I've always wanted to** go there.

Practice B
I'd like to visit China.
So would I. **I wish** I could go there some time.

I've often dreamed of visiting Australia.
So have I. **If only** I could afford to go there.

Practice C
Wouldn't it be lovely to go round the world?
It would indeed. **I've always wanted to** do something like that.

Haven't you always wanted to go to some exotic place like India?
I have indeed. **I've often dreamed of** going somewhere like that.

These facts show how badly the government has done in the last five years.

Production is **DOWN**.
Your standard of living is **DOWN**.
The value of our exports is **DOWN**.
The number of new houses built is **DOWN**.
The number of new schools built is **DOWN**.
Our aid to the Third World is **DOWN**.

Unemployment is **UP**.
The cost of living is **UP**.
The value of our imports is **UP**.
The number of homeless people is **UP**.
House prices are **UP**.
Taxes are **UP**.

Vote for a better government and a better life.

Vote
DEMOCRATIC.

Hope

Expressing hope
I (only/just) hope . . .
Let's hope . . .
Here's hoping . . .!

Practice A
Our standard of living has gone down, hasn't it?
Yes. **I hope** it goes up again soon.

Taxes have gone up, haven't they?
Yes. **Here's hoping** they'll go down again soon.

Practice B
Why has production gone down again?
I don't know, but **let's hope** we can produce more goods next year.

Why have taxes gone up again?
I don't know, but **here's hoping** we can reduce taxes next year.

Practice C
I see house prices are up again.
Yes, I know. **I only hope** they don't go any higher.

I see the standard of living's falling again.
Yes, I know. **I just hope** it doesn't fall any further.

World Cup—Final Stages

Group 1	Pts	Group 2	Pts
Brazil	6	West Germany	6
Italy	4	Argentina	4
Sweden	2	Russia	1
North Korea	0	Zaire	1

Brazil and Italy qualify.

West Germany and Argentina qualify.

Group 3	Pts	Group 4	Pts
Holland	4	Poland	5
Mexico	4	Peru	4
Uruguay	2	Spain	2
Scotland	2	Chile	1

Holland and Mexico qualify.

Poland and Peru qualify.

Quarter finals		Semi finals		Final	
Brazil	2	Brazil	3		
Mexico	0				
				Brazil	2
Holland	3	Holland	1		
Italy	2				
West Germany	2	West Germany	2		
Peru	1				
				West Germany	0
Poland	1	Argentina	0		
Argentina	3				

Regret

Feeling sorry

It's unfortunate/sad (that) . . .
Unfortunately/Sadly . . .
I'm afraid . . .
What/It's/Isn't it a (great) shame/pity (that . . .).
I'm sorry (that) . . .
I regret . . .
I wish . . . had/hadn't . . .
I'm/I was sad to hear/see/learn (that) . . .

Practice A
Boris supports Russia.
I'm afraid they didn't qualify for the quarter finals.

Jan supports Holland.
What a pity they lost in the semi finals.

Practice B
I wish I'd seen West Germany beat Argentina.
Yes, **I'm sorry** I didn't see that match.

I wish I'd seen Brazil beat Mexico.
Yes, **I regret** not having seen that game.

Practice C
How does Maria feel about Argentina being beaten?
She thinks **it's unfortunate.**

How does Juan feel about Mexico being beaten?
He thinks **it's a great shame.**

Worry

Asking what the matter is
What's up/wrong/the matter (with . . .)?
(Is) anything wrong/the matter?
What's/Is something worrying you?
What's on your mind?
What's up?

Describing worries
(Well/Yes,) . . . (actually).
(Well/Yes,) I'm (a bit/rather/very) worried about . . .
I'm worried sick (about . . .).
I can't help worrying about . . .

Keeping worries to oneself
Oh, it's nothing (really).
(No,) I'm OK, thanks.
I'd rather not talk about it, if you don't mind.

Reassuring someone
There's/That's nothing to worry/get upset about.
Don't worry.
Not to worry.
Cheer up. (. . ., I'm sure.)

Practice A
Oh dear!
What's the matter?
Oh, it's nothing really.

Oh dear!
Is anything wrong?
Well, I've got money problems, **actually.**

Practice B
I can't help worrying about money.
What's up?
I'm £100 overdrawn.
Don't worry. So am I.

I'm rather worried about our car.
What's the matter with it?
It's broken down.
Not to worry. Ours is always breaking down.

1.30 **This Time Lucky** 20-1
Good Chance 25-1
Apollo 5-2 fav

2.00 **Miss Blandish** 33-1
Expresso 20-1
Lord Kelly 25-1   fav: **Mr Money** 6-4

2.30 **Irish King** 2-1 fav
Oxford Boy 5-1
Red Admiral 20-1

3.00 **Northern Prince** 18-1
Lovely Lucy 25-1
Sebastian 20-1   fav: **Harry Ramsden** 2-1

3.30 **Quicksilver** 33-1
Tom Thumb 25-1
Billy the Kid 11-4 fav

4.00 **Big Jim** 18-1
Rebel Runner 30-1
Keep Going 9-2 fav

4.30 **First Away** 2-1 fav
That's The One 11-4
Roman Emperor 3-1

5.00 **The Saint** 25-1
Fast Finish 20-1
Whisky 33-1   fav: **Southern Rose** 3-1

Surprise

Expressing surprise
I'm (very) surprised/It's (very) surprising (to hear/see/learn) (that . . .).
I didn't expect . . . to . . .
That *does* surprise me.
That/This *is* a surprise.
(Did it) really?
It didn't, did it?
I don't believe it!
What a surprise/How surprising!
Good Lord/Heavens!
Fancy that!

Not being surprised
Oh, did it?
I'm not surprised.
That's (not very/hardly) surprising (, is it?)
That doesn't surprise me.
(Well,) I (rather) expected . . .
(Well,) it was only to be expected (, wasn't it?)

Practice A
I'm surprised that Northern Prince won the three o'clock.
Yes, the odds were eighteen to one.

I didn't expect Tom Thumb **to** come second in the three-thirty.
No, the odds were twenty-five to one.

Practice B
Lord Kelly came third in the two o'clock.
Really? That *does* **surprise me.**

The Saint won the five o'clock.
It didn't, did it? I didn't expect it **to** win.

Americans to develop
neutron bomb

MPs give themselves
pay rise

Government to build more
nuclear power plants

Britain to cut defence spending

Oil companies to ration
petrol supplies

Unions to refuse pay controls

Government to allow pubs
to stay open all day

Firemen to strike

Museums to charge for entry

Chancellor to put price
of cigarettes up

Scientists to use dogs
for medical research

Approval and disapproval

Expressing approval
I approve of . . .
I'm in favour of . . .
I think it's a (jolly) good thing that . . :
I think . . . is/are (quite) right to . . .

Expressing disapproval
I don't approve of . . .
I'm not in favour of . . .
I think it's terrible/awful that . . .
I think . . . is/are (quite) wrong to . . .

Asking if someone else agrees
Do you?/Don't you?/Are you?/Aren't you?

Expressing agreement
Yes, I approve/disapprove of it too.
Yes, I'm in favour of/against it too.
Yes, I think it's a good/bad thing too.

Expressing disagreement
Oh (no), I don't agree with you. I think/don't think . . . should . . .
Well, I am/do/'m not/don't actually.

Practice A
I approve of the Chancellor putting the price of cigarettes up. **Don't you?**
Yes, I'm in favour of it too.

I'm in favour of oil companies rationing petrol supplies. **Aren't you?**
Oh no, I don't agree with you. I don't think they **should** ration them.

Practice B
I don't approve of the Government building more nuclear power plants. **Do you?**
No, I'm against it too.

I'm not in favour of museums charging for entry. **Are you?**
Well, I am actually. I think they **should** charge for it.

CHICAGO
"A triumph"—Guardian

CHICAGO
"There hasn't been a musical like this for a long time"—Financial Times

CHICAGO
"A super evening's entertainment"—Sunday Express

CHICAGO
"An undoubted success"—Daily Telegraph

GLOO JOO
"The most hilarious play for years"—Financial Times

LOVE'S LABOUR'S LOST
"A perfect performance"
—Guardian

JOKING APART
"Sparkles with wit"—News of the World

AIN'T MISBEHAVIN
"A smash hit"—Daily Mail

CLOUDS
"Michael Frayn's funniest play"—Daily Telegraph

DEATHTRAP
"Very exciting"—Financial Times

WHOSE LIFE IS IT ANYWAY?
West End Theatre Award for
BEST PLAY OF THE YEAR
"A memorable play. I urge you to see it"—Guardian

ONCE A CATHOLIC
"Makes you shake with laughter"—Guardian

THE CHURCHILL PLAY
"Superbly acted"—Guardian

Praise and criticism

Inviting comment
What did you think of . . .?

Praising
(I think/thought) it is/was first rate/excellent/brilliant/superb/
(very) good.
(It's) not bad at all.
It's/It was (very) funny/exciting/well acted/well produced.
It's the best . . . I've seen for a long time.
It's the best . . . I've ever seen.

Modified praising
Parts are/were . . ., but on the whole . . .
Most of it was . . ., but some parts were . . .
It was quite good on the whole.
I've seen worse (. . .).
(It's) not bad.

Criticizing
I didn't enjoy it (at all).
I didn't think much of it (, I'm afraid/myself).
I didn't think much of it. (I'm afraid/myself).
It wasn't very good (, actually).
It was the worst . . . I've seen for a long time.
It was too/rather/a bit boring/long etc. . . .
It wasn't (very/at all) . . .

Practice A
What did you think of *Joking Apart?*
I thought it was brilliant. It was very funny.

What did you think of *The Churchill Play?*
I didn't enjoy it. It was a bit boring.

Practice B
I went to see *Chicago* last night. **It's the best** musical **I've ever seen.**
Do you think so? **I didn't think much of it myself.**

I went to see *Clouds* last night. **It was rather boring.**
Do you think so? **I thought it was very funny.**

Theatre Fire
Who was to blame?

The enquiry into the fire at the Playhouse Theatre last November ended yesterday. Twenty-one people died in the fire, which started in the kitchen of the Theatre Restaurant and spread quickly through the building. The fire was not the fault of any one person alone, but many different people were responsible. The enquiry named these people.

Ken Greenwood
cook – allowed a frying pan to catch fire

Sarah Calverly
waitress – threw water on the fat

Michael Larner
restaurant manager – did not call the fire brigade

Derek Singleton
attendant – locked the main exit door

Keith Stanton
managing director – did nothing about fire prevention

Linda Elton
theatre manager – did not check the fire extinguishers

Alan Barrett
head of the fire brigade – did not inspect the building

Peter Chadwick
builder – broke the safety rules

Stephen Lambert
architect – ignored the risk of fire

Blame

Asking who is to blame
Who's/was to blame?/Is/Was . . . to blame (for . . .)?
Who's/was responsible (for . . .)?/Is/Was . . . responsible (for . . .)?
Whose fault is/was it?/Is/Was it . . .'s fault?
Is anyone to blame?

Saying who is to blame
. . . is/was to blame (for . . .).
. . . is/was responsible (for . . .).
It was . . .'s fault (that . . .).
. . . should/shouldn't have (. . .)
. . . ought (not) to have (. . .)

Not blaming anyone
Nobody was (directly/entirely) to blame (but . . .).
It wasn't anyone's/any one person's/my fault.
I'm not blaming anyone in particular (but . . .).
Something ought to/should have been done . . .

Practice A
Was the attendant **to blame?**
Well, **nobody was entirely to blame, but it was his fault that** the
main exit door was locked.

Was the architect **responsible?**
Well, **it wasn't any one person's fault, but he was to blame for**
ignoring the risk of fire.

Practice B
Something should have been done about fire prevention, but it wasn't.
Yes, the managing director **was to blame for** that.

The safety rules **oughtn't to have been broken,** but they were.
Yes, **that was** the builder's **fault.**

Practice C
What did Michael Larner do wrong?
He didn't call the fire brigade when he **ought to have.**

What did Sarah Calverly do wrong?
She threw water on the fat when she **shouldn't have.**

"LUNA"
WATCH
KEEPS PERFECT
TIME

SPARKLE
WASHING
POWDER

Removes
All Stains

BREEZE
HAIR DRYER

DRYS HAIR
FAST

GREEN
FINGERS
SWEET PEA
SEEDS

produce
flowers
in
6
weeks

'THE OXFORD'
SCISSORS

CUT
ANY
MATERIAL

LIGHTS
EVERY
TIME

SUPERSTICK
glue

sticks
everything

LONG
LIFE
TORCH
BATTERY

LASTS
FOR
60
HOURS

GRIPEASY
plastic gloves

protect
your
hands

Complaints

Making a complaint
I have a complaint to make about . . .
I want to make a complaint about . . .
I'm not (at all) satisfied with . . .
I'd like you to do something about . . .
It's/They're (absolutely) no good/useless (. . .)
It doesn't/They don't work . . .
It says here . . . but it doesn't/they don't.
It/They just isn't/aren't . . . (enough).

Practice A
I have a complaint to make about this battery.
What's wrong with it?
It doesn't last for sixty hours.

I'm not satisfied with this washing powder.
What's wrong with it?
It doesn't remove all stains.

Practice B
What's wrong with this watch?
It doesn't work. It says here it keeps perfect time, **but it doesn't.**

What's wrong with these gloves?
They're no good. It says here they protect your hands, **but they don't.**

Practice C
What are your new scissors like?
They just aren't sharp **enough.**

What's your new hair drier like?
It just doesn't dry fast **enough.**

RULES FOR TENANTS AT THIS HOSTEL

Tenants must not:

have parties
play records after midnight
have a bath after midnight
hang up their clothes to dry in the
    bathroom
bring dogs into the hostel
park their cars in front of the garage
    doors
leave rubbish in the garden

Tenants must:

pay the rent every Thursday
clean the corridor
put the hall light out at night
wash up after each meal
only use the public telephone in the
    corridor
clean out the bath, basin, washing
    machine after use
put out their rubbish for collection
    every Wednesday

Apologies

Apologizing

I'm (so/very/extremely/awfully/terribly/really) sorry (. . .).
I (do) apologize (for . . .).
Please accept my apologies.
How . . . of me! I'm sorry.

Accepting an apology

That's/It's all right/OK (. . .).
It doesn't matter (this time but/as long as . . .).
. . . but don't do it/don't let it happen again, will you?
. . . but see that it doesn't happen again, won't you?

Rejecting an apology

It's easy to say sorry, but . . .
Saying sorry just isn't enough, I'm afraid . . .
It's too late to apologize now!

Practice A
Was it you who played records after midnight?
I'm terribly sorry. I didn't know I wasn't allowed to play them.

Was it you who didn't put the hall light out?
I do apologize. I didn't know I had to put it out.

Practice B
I'm very sorry I brought a dog into the building.
It doesn't matter, but don't do it again, will you?

I apologize for having a bath after midnight.
That's all right.

I'm awfully sorry I didn't pay the rent on Thursday.
That's OK, as long as you pay it next week.

Good wishes and friendly enquiries

Good wishes
(I hope you) have a good/nice . . .
(I hope you) enjoy it/yourself/yourselves.

Friendly enquiries
(Have you) had a good/nice . . .?
Did you have a good/nice . . .?
What was . . . like?
How was . . .?
Did you enjoy . . .?

Saying if you enjoyed something
(Yes, I/we did, thank you.) It was lovely/(very) good/nice/great/fun.
It was all right.
I/We didn't enjoy it much, actually. . . .

Practice A
I'm going to Italy tomorrow.
Well, **have a good** trip.
Thank you.

I'm going to a concert this evening.
Well, **I hope you enjoy it.**
Thank you.

Practice B
Did you have a good holiday in Hong Kong?
Yes, we did, thank you. It was lovely.

How was your weekend in Folkestone?
Well, **I didn't enjoy it very much, actually.** It rained all the time.

Compliments

Fishing for compliments
What do you think of my (new) . . . (, then)?
I think . . . suits me. Don't you?
Do you like my (new) . . .?

Complimenting someone on their clothes
I like . . .
What a . . .!
That/Those . . . is/are nice.
. . . look/looks nice (on you).
That's a/Those are nice . . .
You (do) look nice (in . . .).
. . . (*really*) suits/*does* suit you.

Answering a compliment
Thank you/Thanks. (I'm glad you like it/them.)
(It's) nice of you to say so.
Mm, it is . . ., isn't it?
Really? I'm not sure (about it/them), actually.

Practice A
I like your handbag.
Thank you.

Those jeans **are nice.**
Thanks. I'm glad you like them.

Practice B
Do you like my new coat?
Yes, very much. **It really suits you.** Where did you get it?
At a boutique, actually.

What do you think of my new jeans?
They look nice on you. Where did you get them?
In the market, actually.

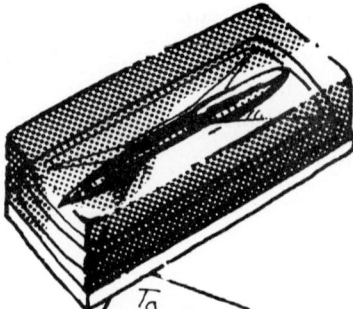

Thanks

Thanking

Thank you (for . . .).
Thank you very much (indeed) (for . . .).
Thanks (a lot/very much) (for . . .).
Many thanks (for . . .).
I'm very grateful (to you for . . .).
Thank you *etc.* I was pleased/delighted with it/them.
        It's/They're lovely/very nice/just
        what I wanted.
        It was (very) kind/nice/thoughtful
        of you (to . . .).
        You shouldn't have (. . .).

Responding to thanks

That's all right/OK.
Not at all.
(It's/It was) a pleasure.
Any time.
Don't mention it.
You're welcome.
I hope you like it.

Practice A
I've brought this present for you, Daniel.
Oh, a watch. **Thank you very much indeed.**

Here's a present for you, Laura.
Oh, some wine. **Thanks very much.**

Practice B
Thanks a lot for the umbrella, Andrew. **It's just what I wanted.**
Oh, **don't mention it.**

Thank you for the vase, David. **It was very kind of you.**
That's all right. I hope you like it.

pot¹ /pɒt/ *n* **1** round vessel of earthenware, metal or glass, for holding liquids or solids, for cooking things in, etc; contents of such a vessel: *a 'jam-pot; eat a whole pot of jam; a 'teapot; a 'coffee-pot; a 'flower-pot; a 'chamber-pot.* ⇨ the *nn* forming the first element of such compounds. **2** (phrases and provs) **go to pot,** (sl) be ruined or destroyed. **keep the 'pot boiling,** earn enough money to buy one's food, etc; keep sth, eg a children's game, going briskly. **take ,pot 'luck,** whatever is available (without choice); whatever is being prepared for a meal: *Come home with me and take pot luck.* **the ,pot calling the ,kettle 'black,** the accuser having the same fault as the accused. **3** (colloq) large sum: *make a pot/pots of money.* **4 a big pot,** (colloq) an important person. **5** (colloq) prize in an athletic contest, esp a silver cup: *all the pots he won when he was young.* **6** (sl) marijuana. **7** (compounds) **'pot-belly** *n* (person with a) large, prominent belly. **,pot-'bellied** *adj* (of a person) having a pot-belly; (of a stove) having a rounded container in which fuel, eg wood, burns. **'pot-boiler** *n* book, picture, etc produced merely to bring in money. **'pot-bound** *adj* (of a plant) having roots that have filled its pot. **'pot-boy, 'pot-man** /-mən/ (*pl* -men) *nn* (hist) one who helps in a public house by filling pots with beer, etc. **'pot hat** *n* (sl) bowler hat. **'pot-head** *n* (sl) habitual marijuana user. **'pot-herb** *n* plant, etc whose leaves or stems, or whose roots or tubers, are used in cooking. **'pot-hole** *n* (a) hole in a road made by rain and traffic. (b) deep cylindrical hole worn in rock (eg in limestone caves) by water. **'pot-holer** *n* person who explores pot-holes in caves. **'pot-hook** *n* (a) hook, often S-shaped, which can be raised or lowered on a metal bar, for holding pots, etc over a fireplace. (b) curved or wavy stroke made by children when learning to write their letters. **'pot-house** *n* (old use) low-class public house; ale-house: *pot-house manners,* vulgar manners. **'pot-hunter** *n* (a) sportsman who shoots anything he comes across, thinking only of food for the pot or profit. (b) person who takes part in contests merely for the sake of the prizes. ⇨ **5** above. **'pot roast** *n* beef, etc browned in a pot and cooked slowly with very little water. **'pot-shot** *n* shot aimed at a bird or animal that is near, so that careful aim is not needed; random shot. **'pot-trained** *adj* (of a small child) trained to use a chamber pot.

pot² /pɒt/ *vt,vi* (-tt-) **1** [VP6A] put (meat, fish paste, etc) in a pot to preserve it: *potted shrimps/ ham.* **2** [VP6A,15B] **pot (up),** plant in a flower-pot: *pot (up) chrysanthemum cuttings.* **3** [VP6A] kill with a pot-shot: *pot a rabbit;* [VP3A] **pot at,** shoot at: *~ a hare.* **4** (billiards) drive a ball into a pocket. **5** (colloq) put (a baby) on a chamber-pot. **pot·able** /'pəʊtəbl/ *adj* fit to drink.

pot·ash /'pɒtæʃ/ *n* [U] common name for various potassium salts, used in the manufacture of fertilizers, soap, and various chemicals.

po·tass·ium /pə'tæsɪəm/ *n* [U] soft, shining, white metallic element (symbol **K**), vital to all living matter, occurring in the form of mineral salts and in rocks.

po·ta·tion /pəʊ'teɪʃn/ *n* (liter) drink.

po·tato /pə'teɪtəʊ/ *n* (*pl* ~es /-təʊz/) plant with rounded tubers eaten as a vegetable; one of the tubers: *baked ~es; mashed ~(es); ~ soup;* (US) *~ chips* (= GB *crisps*). ⇨ the illus at vegetable. **,sweet '~,** tropical plant with long tuberous roots

used for food. **'~ beetle,** beetle that destroys the leaves of ~ plants.

po·teen /pɒ'tiːn/ *n* [U] Irish whisky from an illicit still.

po·tent /'pəʊtnt/ *adj* (not of persons or machines) powerful: *~ reasons/arguments/charms/drugs/ remedies;* (of males) not sexually impotent. **~·ly** *adv* **po·tency** /-nsɪ/ *n*

po·ten·tate /'pəʊtnteɪt/ *n* powerful person; monarch; ruler.

po·ten·tial /pə'tenʃl/ *adj* **1** that can or may come into existence or action: *~ wealth/resources; ~ energy* (waiting to be released); *the ~ sales of a new book.* **2** *~ mood,* (gram) indicating possibility. □ *n* **1** [C] that which is ~; possibility; [U] what sb or sth is capable of: *He hasn't realized his full ~ yet.* **2** (gram) *~ mood.* **3** (electr) energy of an electric charge, expressed in volts: *a current of high ~.* **~·ly** /-ʃəlɪ/ *adv* a *~ly rich country,* eg one with rich but undeveloped natural resources. **~·ity** /pə,tenʃɪ'ælətɪ/ *n* (*pl* -ties) power or quality which is ~, and needs development; latent capacity: *a situation/a country with great potentialities.*

pother /'pɒðə(r)/ *n* trouble; commotion.

po·tion /'pəʊʃn/ *n* [C] dose of liquid medicine or poison, or of sth used in magic: *a 'love ~.*

pot-pourri /,pəʊ 'pʊərɪ: *US:* pə'riː/ *n* **1** mixture of dried rose-petals and spices, kept in a jar for its perfume. **2** musical or literary medley.

pot·sherd /'pɒtʃɜːd/ *n* broken piece of pottery (esp in archaeology).

pot·tage /'pɒtɪdʒ/ *n* (old use) thick soup.

potted /'pɒtɪd/ *adj* **1** ⇨ **pot**². **2** (of a book, etc) inadequately summarized: *a ~ version of a classical novel.*

pot·ter¹ /'pɒtə(r)/ (US = **put·ter** /'pʌtər/) *vi* [VP2A,C] **1** work with little energy; move about from one little job to another: *~ing about in the garden.* **2** waste (time) in ~ing: *~ away a whole afternoon.* **~·er** *n* person who ~s.

pot·ter² /'pɒtə(r)/ *n* maker of pots. **~'s wheel,** horizontal revolving disc on which pots are shaped.

pot·tery *n* (*pl* -ries) [U] earthenware; pots; [C] **~'s workshop. the Potteries,** district in Staffordshire, England where **~**y is the chief industry.

a potter's wheel

potty¹ /'pɒtɪ/ *adj* (-ier, -iest) (GB dated colloq) **1** petty; unimportant; insignificant: *~ little details/ jobs.* **2** *~ (about sb/sth),* (of a person) foolish, crazy: *She's quite ~, mad. He's ~ about his new gramophone.*

potty² /'pɒtɪ/ *n* (*pl* -ties) child's chamber-pot.

pouch /paʊtʃ/ *n* **1** small bag carried in the pocket (*a to'bacco-~*) or fastened to the belt (a soldier's *,ammu'nition-~*). **2** bag-like formation, eg that in which a female kangaroo carries her young. ⇨ the illus at large. **3** puffy area of skin, eg under the eyes of a sick or old person. □ *vt* **1** [VP6A] put into a ~. **2** [VP6A] make (part of a dress, etc) like a ~;

Questions about meaning

Asking what a word means
What's (a/to) . . .?
What (on earth) does . . . mean?
What's the meaning of (the word) . . .?
I don't understand (the word) . . .

Practice A
What's a 'pot-hole'?
It's a hole in a road made by rain and traffic.

What does 'to potter' **mean?**
It means to work with little energy.

Practice B
What on earth does 'potty' **mean?**
It means 'unimportant, foolish or crazy'.
So 'She's potty about Robert Redford' means 'she's crazy about him'.
That's right.

I don't understand the word 'potential'.
It means 'that can or may come into existence'.
So 'He hasn't realized his full potential 'means' he hasn't done what he's capable of'.
That's right.

Questions about words for people and things

Asking for words about people
What's the word for a person/someone who . . .?
What do you call a person/someone who . . .?
What is a person/someone who . . . called?
What word do you use for a person/someone who . . .?

Asking for words about things
What's the name of the thing/stuff you use for/to . . .?
What do you call stuff/a thing you use for/to . . .?
What's the word for something you . . . (with)?

Giving a word
(Oh,) we call him/her/it/that . . .
(Oh,) that's called . . . (, isn't it/I think).
(Oh,) you (must) mean . . .
It's on the tip of my tongue. Oh yes, . . .

Not giving a word
(I) haven't a clue (, I'm afraid).
(I've) no idea.
I don't know the word for that (, I'm afraid).

Practice A
What do you call someone who watches a race?
A spectator.

What's the word for a person who sees something happen?
I haven't a clue, I'm afraid.

Practice B
What do you call stuff for baking cakes?
Oh, **you mean** flour.

What's the word for something you cut wood **with?**
Oh, **you mean** a saw.

Questions about words for situations

Asking for a word
What do you call/What is it called when . . .?
What word do you use to talk about . . .?
Is there/Do you have a word that means . . .?

Giving a word
We say . . .
That's (called) (a) . . .
(I think) we/they call it/that (a) . . .
(A) . . . (, I think).
(Oh,) you (must) mean (a) . . .
It's on the tip of my tongue. Oh yes, . . .

Not giving a word
(I) haven't a clue (, I'm afraid).
(I've) no idea.
I don't know the word for that (, I'm afraid).

Practice A
What is it called when one car goes past another?
I haven't a clue, I'm afraid.

What word do you use to talk about a collection of paintings that
people can go and see?
I've no idea.

Practice B
What word do you use to talk about two people getting married in a
church?
We call that a wedding.

Is there a word that means two teams score the same number of
goals?
That's a draw.

Meeting someone for the first time

Meeting someone you know

Not hearing what someone says to you

Wanting someone to move out of the way

Warning someone of danger

Someone sneezing

About to start drinking

Wanting someone to come into your room

Deciding not to buy something

Questions about usage

Asking how a phrase is used
When would you say . . .?
When should I use the phrase/word . . .?

Asking what to say
What do you say when . . .?
What's the right/best thing to say when . . .?

Practice A
What do you say when you decide not to buy something?
You say 'I'll leave it, thank you.'

What's the right thing to say when you don't hear what someone
says to you?
You say 'Pardon?'

Practice B
When would you say 'How do you do'?
When I meet someone for the first time.

When should I use the word 'Cheers'?
When you're about to start drinking.

Appendix for the teacher

This Appendix contains suggestions for more open-ended practice of each communicative function, keys to illustrations, notes on language items where necessary, and cross references to *Cue for a Drill* for a further structural practice.

Section 1 Identification, Description and Reports

Identification of people   9
Key to the illustrations: *Actors* Charlie Chaplin, Dustin Hoffman, Clint Eastwood; *Actresses* Marlene Dietrich, Sophia Loren, Jane Fonda; *Singers* Joan Baez, Elvis Presley, Maria Callas; *Politicians* Mrs Ghandi, Mrs Thatcher, Edward Kennedy.

Further functional practice: Students are asked to bring to the class a photograph of themselves as a baby or child. They try to identify each other from the photographs.

Identification on the telephone   11
Note that Practice C involves three speakers.

Further functional practice: Students work in pairs, acting out dialogues in which they ask to speak to famous people they would like to hold a conversation with.

Identification of things   13
Key to the illustrations: *Cars* Volkswagen, Citroen, Rolls-Royce; *Planes* Boeing 707, Trident, Concorde; *Birds* owl, eagle, flamingo; *Instruments* clarinet, trumpet, saxophone.

Further functional practice: Students are asked to bring to the class 3 pictures or objects, each connected with their own interests or hobby. If they like gardening, they might bring 3 pictures of flowers. If they like cooking, 3 pictures of foodstuffs. The class tries to identify the objects. Alternatively, one might play the game of 'silly pictures'. For example:

What's this?

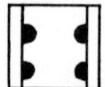

(I'm not sure, but it may be) a worm sliding over a razor blade/a giraffe going past a window/a bear climbing a tree.

Description of people   15
Relevant vocabulary items: *Build* tall, short, thin, slim, skinny, plump, fat, stout, stocky, well-built; *Age* in his/her teens, in his/her (early/mid/late) forties etc.; *Hair* fair, dark, grey, white, curly, straight, wavy, long, short, shoulder-length, fringe, bald; *Colouring* black,

coloured, dark-skinned, pale, fair; *Clothing* wear, be (dressed) in, have (got) on; *Features* beard, moustache, bushy eyebrows, clean-shaven, spectacles, glasses, dark glasses.

Further functional practice: The students are each asked to bring (or the teacher provides) a picture of a well-known person. The class then try to describe these people. Alternatively, students can play a game in which a student gives a description of someone in the room and the others try to guess who he/she is talking about.

Further structural practice: *Cue for a Drill* p. 11, have, have got; p. 97, often, always, never.

Description of things 17
Relevant vocabulary items: *Size* big, large, small; *Shape* long, square, narrow, round, oval, triangular, diamond-shaped; *Material* woollen, leather, cloth, cotton, silk, gold, silver, nylon, plastic; *Features* striped, pattern(ed), label, shoulder strap, bracelet.

Further functional practice: Each student is asked to produce something (e.g. a wallet, ear-rings) for the others to describe.

Description of a process 19
Further functional practice: One or two students describe processes which they are familiar with but which the other students may not know much about. The process might be a manufacturing process, the making of an object or a scientific experiment. The other students can ask questions about the process.

Further structural practice: *Cue for a Drill* p.63, passive voice; p.117, after, when, before.

Messages 21
Further functional practice: Each student is asked who was the last person they spoke to before coming into the class, or the first person they spoke to that morning. Students report what was said to them.

Further structural practice: *Cue for a Drill* p.71, Drill A, reporting statements.

Reports 23
Further functional practice: Cut out some suitable comic strips (e.g. *Peanuts*) and get the class to describe what the characters are doing and report what they say. If students are sufficiently advanced, ask them to relate a real topical negotiation (local, union or international).

Further structural practice: *Cue for a Drill* p.73, Drill B, reporting complaints and suggestions.

Section 2   Information

Requests for information   25
Further functional practice: Students should be asked to bring a local
newspaper with an Entertainments Guide section. Working in pairs, one
student plays the role of a stranger in town, asking for information about
what's on, while the other supplies the information.

Checking information   27
Further functional practice: Ask the students to imagine they are, for
example, buying a car, renting a flat, or deciding whether to accept the
offer of a job. Students work in pairs, one student checking whether the
car/flat/job etc. has all the desired qualities. The student supplying the
information is either free to invent the details, or is given a role-card
prepared by the teacher.

Reactions to information   29
Further functional practice: Cut out some headlines or short news items
from newspapers and distribute them round the class. Each student then
summarizes the information in one or two sentences or expands the
headline into a sentence for a partner to react to. *The Guinness Book of
Records* (Guinness Superlatives Ltd.) and *The Book of Lists* (Corgi Books)
are other useful sources of out-of-the-way information.

Agreeing with and correcting statements of fact   31
Further functional practice: Write on the board a series of general
knowledge statements with a missing item, e.g. . . . is the longest river
in the world. The students are asked in turn to complete a statement
orally. The items should be challenging enough to induce errors which
can be corrected by the other students.

Further structural practice: *Cue for a Drill* p.45, Drill C; p.125, Drill A.

Explanations   33
Further functional practice: Ask the students to rate the popularity of
their own national or local government and explain why they happen to
be popular or unpopular. Or, if you wish to steer clear of politics, get
them to explain other news items of topical interest.

Section 3   Opinions and decisions

Opinions   35

Further functional practice: Students are given more topics or think of
other topics for themselves e.g. looking after old people, nuclear power,
the race problem, the distribution of wealth, drugs, divorce, abortion.
They ask each other for their opinions on these topics.

Agreement and disagreement with opinions   37

Further functional practice: Students ask each other for their opinions on
various topics (as under Opinions) and agree or disagree with each other.

Predictions   39

Further functional practice: Students discuss what the world will be like
in 50 or 100 years' time. Will there still be poverty? Will people have
more leisure? Will pollution destroy the environment? Will there be a
nuclear war or a nuclear energy disaster in the next 50 or 100 years?

Further structural practice: *Cue for a Drill* p.89, will, be going to.

Imagination   41

Further functional practice: Ask the students to imagine what it would
be like to be a dictator of the whole world. What would they do?

Further structural practice: *Cue for a Drill* p.69 Exercise C, would.

Decisions   43

Further functional practice: The students are spending an evening in
London (or in the place where they really are). They have to decide how
they are going to spend the evening and tell the teacher, or tell each
other, what they decide to do. If possible a list of events and
entertainments should be available for the students.

Intentions   45

Further functional practice: Students discuss their own intentions as to
their education and training and applying for a (new) job.

Further structural practice: *Cue for a Drill* p.37, be going to, will be
doing.

Plans   47

Further functional practice: Students discuss their own holiday plans in
detail.
Further structural practice: *Cue for a Drill* p.41, Drill A.

Section 4   Getting people to do things

Requests for things   49
Further functional practice: Ask each student to write a short shopping list. Students work in pairs, one playing the role of a customer, the other the role of a shop assistant.

Requests to do things   51
Further functional practice: Ask each student to draw up a short list of things he/she has to do, as in the second half of the visual, and to ask other members of the class to do the things for them.

Permission   53
Further functional practice: The students ask each other's permission to borrow e.g. a book/bicycle; or they ask the teacher's permission to e.g. open the window/leave early/play a game.

Further structural practice: *Cue for a Drill* p.51, can, can't, be allowed to.

Suggestions   55
Further functional practice: Suggest to the class that there should be a class outing one Saturday, or one evening, then ask them to suggest what you should all do, or where you should go.

Further structural practice: *Cue for a Drill* p.61 Drill A, Let's . . ., shall we?; p.91, Drill A, Why don't you . . .?

Advice   57
Further functional practice: Ask students to think of a large item they would like to buy (e.g. a car, a motorcycle, a watch, etc.). They then ask the rest of the class for their advice as to which make to buy.

Further structural practice: *Cue for a Drill* p.59, had better, ought to, should.

Recommendations   59
Further functional practice: The students should make recommendations to one another on where to spend their next holiday, either by drawing on their own experience, or by using travel brochures provided by the teacher.

Further structural practice: *Cue for a Drill* p.119, Drill C.

Reminders; Warnings   61, 63
Further functional practice: Ask which students are going out for the evening or going away for a longer period and which students are

planning to do potentially dangerous things e.g. driving a long distance, riding a motor-bike, going climbing or sailing, fixing something electrical. Get the class to give the appropriate reminders and/or warnings.

Further structural practice: *Cue for a Drill* p.55, Drill B, in case.

Insistence, threats and promises 65

Further functional practice: If the students are adults ask them to imagine that they are (either individually or in groups) the spokesman for a trade union. They should draw up a list of things that they would like to see improved in their conditions of work. If the class is sufficiently advanced, you can extend the promising function by showing them how to bargain. (E.g. We will . . . if you will . . . .) Then get them to conduct a mini-role-play in industrial negotiations. With younger students, one might get them to list the things they would like changed in their present education system.

Section 5   Offers, acceptance and refusal

Invitations 67

Further functional practice: Ask each student to invite another member of the class to an actual event or private occasion.

Further structural practice: *Cue for a Drill* p.75, Drill C, Would you like to . . .?

Offers of food and drink 69

Further functional practice: If it is not possible to have an actual meal, picnic or drinks with the students, then collect empty chocolate boxes, cigarette packets, wine bottles etc. and get the students to offer things to each other.

Further structural practice: *Cue for a Drill* p.53, Drill C.

Offers of help 71

Further functional practice: Ask the students to imagine they are in charge of organizing something, e.g. redecorating the classroom, starting a class newspaper, a school dance or picnic etc. Get them to draw up a list of things that need doing. Individual students then offer their help in getting the job done.

Further structural practice: *Cue for a Drill* p.61, Drill C, I'll . . ., shall I?

Refusals 73
Further functional practice: The teacher imagines that he/she is the dictator of a country, or the autocratic head of some organization, and draws up a list of laws/rules that are totally absurd. He/She explains the situation to the class and gets them to refuse to obey these rules.

Section 6 Feelings

Pleasure and annoyance 75
Further functional practice: Students think of bits of news they would like to hear (e.g. Next Monday is a public holiday/Everyone is invited to a party) and bits of news they would not like to hear (e.g. The price of coffee is going up 50%/Everyone has to do an English test tomorrow). Students write down a few examples and then do oral work in pairs, telling each other their news and expressing pleasure or annoyance.

Likes and dislikes 77
Further functional practice: Students say what hobbies, sports, film stars, food etc. they like and ask other students whether they like the same thing too.
Further structural practice: *Cue for a Drill* p.75, Drill B and Exercise B, like, prefer, enjoy; p.79, like, love, enjoy; can't stand, can't bear; be keen on, be fond of.

Preferences 79
Further functional practice: Students ask each other which of two things they prefer, e.g. pop music or classical music, tea or coffee, cats or dogs, red wine or white wine, hot weather or cold weather, living in the town or living in the country, travelling by car or by train, reading a good book or seeing a good film.
Further structural practice: *Cue for a Drill*, p.75, Drill B.

Wanting things 81
Further functional practice: The teacher gives a few examples of things that he/she would like and says why, e.g. 'I'd like a new car because the one I've got breaks down a lot. I want a new coat because the one I've got is very old. I'd also like a pocket calculator because it would be easier to add up your marks.' Students then say what they would like.

Wishes 83
Further functional practice: Students say what they wish would happen. E.g. 'I wish I could play the guitar/If only I had a lot of money/I'd love to travel round the world.'
Further structural practice: *Cue for a Drill* p.103, Drills B and C.

Hope 85
Further functional practice: Students express their hopes on such topics as tomorrow's weather, sports results, exam results or marks, getting a job or promotion, money.

Regret 87
Further functional practice: Students talk about things they regret at present in their own lives, e.g. 'It's a pity I can't go out tonight. Unfortunately I have a lot of homework to do tonight. I regret not having done it at the weekend.'
Further structural practice: *Cue for a Drill* p.49, Drill C, wish.

Worry 89
Further functional practice: Students may be willing to talk about their own worries e.g. about school marks, exams, getting a job, business worries, money worries, health, family problems.

Surprise 91
Further functional practice: Students think of bits of surprising news (e.g. The British have elected a black Prime Minister/Someone has swum across the Atlantic Ocean/North Korea has won the World Cup/The USA, the USSR and China have agreed to give up nuclear weapons). Students write down a few examples and then do oral work in pairs, telling their news and expressing surprise.

Section 7 Right and wrong

Approval and disapproval 93
Further functional practice: The students should think of other bits of news of topical interest and react with approval or disapproval.

Praise and criticism 95
Further functional practice: Ask the students to think of all the films, plays and TV shows they have seen or books they have read recently, and to choose one to praise or criticize for the rest of the class.

Blame   97

Further functional practice: Students discuss who is to blame for e.g. pollution, strikes, unemployment or the high number of road accidents.

Complaints   99

Further functional practice: Each student brings to the class an object he/she has bought and found unsatisfactory, e.g. a pen that doesn't write very well. The student complains about it to a partner who plays the role of a shop assistant. The shop assistant finds out what is wrong and then agrees to give the money back. This activity is best demonstrated by a teacher and a student in front of the class before practice in pairs.

Apologies   101

Further functional practice: 'Accuse' individual students by saying e.g. 'You took my pen and didn't give it back/You didn't do your homework/You were late today/You haven't got your book.' Students apologize and add an excuse, the teacher accepting the apology. Students can do the same in pairs.

Section 8   Being polite

Good wishes and friendly enquiries   103

Further functional practice: Students say what journeys they are going to make or what entertainments or cultural events they are going to attend, and the others express good wishes. Past events can also be the topic, e.g. 'I went to the disco last night.—Did you enjoy it/have a good time?—Yes, thank you.'

Compliments   105

Further functional practice: Students talk about each other's clothes and pay each other compliments.

Thanks   107

Further functional practice: Tell individual students of favours you have done them, e.g. 'I've brought the book you wanted/I've checked this

extra work for you/I've found an English pen-friend for you/I've got
you a ticket for the British library.' Students thank you, and you
acknowledge their thanks. Students can then do the same in pairs.

Section 9   Enquiries about language

Questions about meaning   *109*
Further functional practice: Students can play a game in which members
of one team ask the other team to explain the meanings of words, one
point being scored for a correct explanation. If the word is too difficult
for the questioner himself/herself to explain, then he/she loses a point.

Questions about words for people and things   *111*
Key to the illustrations: *Top row* barrister, kettle, invalid; *Second row*
flour, patient, ink; *Third row* porter, saw, spectator; *Bottom row* shampoo,
witness, spade.

Further functional practice: Students can play a game in which members
of one team ask the other team for a word by supplying the definition,
one point being scored for a correct answer. The questioner must also
know the word or lose a point.

Questions about words for situations   *113*
Key to the illustrations: *Top row* exhibition, sale; *Second row* overtaking,
strike; *Bottom row* draw, wedding.

Further functional practice: As for page 110.

Questions about usage   *115*
Further functional practice: Students can ask more questions about similar
phrases for special situations, e.g. when you leave a party, when you
bump into someone, when someone tries to give you something you
don't want, when you want someone to dance with you.

Index